NAPOLEON

The Life of Napoleon Bonaparte

By James Anderson

Table of Contents

Introduction 2
Chapter 1 Napoleon Bonaparte's Early Years 5
    Early Life and Education 6
    Napoleon Bonaparte's Early Military Career 9
    Chapter Summary 13
    Segue 14
Chapter 2 Napoleon Bonaparte's Premiere Campaign of Italy . 15
    Napoleon Takes Command of the French Army of Italy 16
    Napoleon's First Victories as Commander-in-Chief 19
    The Battle of Lodi 20
    The Army of Italy Enters Milan 21
    Napoleon Besieges Mantua 23
    Defeat at the Second Battle of Bassano 24
    The Fall of Mantua 26
    Chapter Summary 27
    Segue 28
Chapter 3 Napoleon Bonaparte's Expedition to Egypt 29
    The Directory Approves Napoleon's Expedition to Egypt 30
    The British Naval Threat 32
    The French Occupy Cairo 33
    Napoleon Campaigns in Syria 35
    The Siege of Acre 36
    Napoleon Retreats 37
    Aftermath 39
    Chapter Summary 40
    Segue 41

Chapter 4 Napoleon Bonaparte's Rise to Power.........................42
  The Second Coalition...43
  Napoleon's Second Campaign in Italy.................................44
  Napoleon Serves as the First Consul of France....................46
  Why Did Napoleon Put His Hand in His Coat?....................49
  Napoleon Bonaparte's Battle Tactics and Influences............50
  What Did the People and Governments Think of Napoleon
  and Empress Josephine?..52
  Chapter Summary..54
  Segue..54

Chapter 5 The Crowning of an Emperor.....................................55
  The Painting in the Louvre..56
  Napoleon Bonaparte is Crowned Emperor...........................57
  Napoleon's "Grande Armee"..62
  What Did Napoleon Do For France as Emperor?.................64
  Emperor Bonaparte's Greatest Enemies................................66
  Chapter Summary..69
  Segue..70

Chapter 6 A New Empress...71
  Why Did Napoleon Marry Josephine?..................................72
  Why Did Napoleon Separate From Josephine?....................74
  Napoleon's New Marriage...74
  What Was Brewing in Europe During This Time?................76
  Chapter Summary..78
  Segue..79

Chapter 7 Napoleon's Retreat From Moscow..............................80
  Napoleon's Russian Campaign 81
  Chapter Summary..87
  Segue..88

Chapter 8 An Emperor Falls..89
  The War of the Sixth Coalition..90
  The Allies Ask Napoleon for an Armistice............................91
  Invasion of France..93
  Chapter Summary..96
  Segue..97

Chapter 9 The 100 Days **98**
   How Did Napoleon Escape Exile? 99
   Precursory Battles Leading Up to Waterloo 100
   The Battle of Waterloo.. 101
   Chapter Summary 103
   Segue 103

Chapter 10 A Second Exile **104**
   Life on the Island of St. Helena... 105
   How Did Napoleon Bonaparte Die? 107
   Chapter Summary 108
   Segue 108

Conclusion..**109**

Resources..**111**

Introduction

As a history lover, I've always found Napoleon Bonaparte and his long list of failures (as well as his many successes) in both his political and personal life fascinating. I've spent a considerable amount of time researching and merging information for this book, and have learned a lot about one of my favorite historical figures. There is a lot of incorrect information out there about Napoleon Bonaparte, so if you're confused about who he is and the mark that he's made on European history, don't worry — you're not the only one.

In films and articles, Napoleon Bonaparte is often portrayed in ways that are quite "dramatized" or just flat-out wrong, and it's important to me that people know the truth about his life. My aim, in writing this book, is to provide you with that truth so that you may gain clarity and more perspective on what happened.

Napoleon Bonaparte is a well-known figure in history, and it's easy to see why. He led quite a life, starting as an outsider from Corsica and then quickly gaining power as the Emperor of France in 1804. You may already know, though, that Napoleon Bonaparte eventually fell from grace — his failures are what he's most famous for, after all. If you're wondering how he rose to such great power, only to experience such a great fall, then you're not alone. I'm sure a great deal of people out there is as curious as you are.

Napoleon Bonaparte, also known as Napoleon I, made a major impact during the early 19th century. He was born in 1769 on the island of Corsica. He was a French military leader who rose through the ranks quickly, which was surprising because this was an especially chaotic time in France.

Napoleon's fame is mainly tied to the French Revolution, which started in 1787 and lasted through 1799. During this time, he showed he was a very smart and ambitious man (his extreme ambition, however, may have ultimately led to his downfall). By 1799, he had taken control of France in a coup —a big turning point. In just five years, 1804 to be exact, he was able to call himself Emperor.

Napoleon wasn't just a political mastermind. He also led plenty of successful campaigns in wars against groups of European countries and could even expand his empire, taking over a big part of Europe. There are a lot of successes that are worth talking about (and honestly aren't talked about enough) when it comes to Napoleon Bonaparte. I'll certainly be going over his most notable successes throughout this book, so don't worry! In 1812, however, Napoleon tried to invade Russia, which is when things started going awry.

His invasion of Russia turned out to be a major disaster. He had to give up being Emperor of France in 1814 and was soon after exiled to an island called Elba. Surprisingly, he made a comeback in 1815 during the Hundred Days campaign (which we'll be talking about more in-depth later).

His success didn't last long, as many history buffs know, he lost the Battle of Waterloo and was forced to step down from his position of power, and was, once again, exiled to a remote island — this time Saint Helena. This is where Napoleon Bonaparte died in 1821 at the age of 51. His death certainly marked the end of an important period in French and European history. He didn't live a long life, but he did live a full life. This is, perhaps, what makes him so captivating.

All of this happened a very long time ago, so you might be wondering why and how Napoleon Bonaparte left such a lasting mark on European history. Throughout this book, we'll be breaking down the events of his life and delving into his successes and failures as the Emperor of France. If you've been wanting to learn more about

Napoleon Bonaparte and the impact that he left on the world, this may just be the book you've been looking for.

We'll be discussing quite a bit here, including his early life, his 1796 Premiere campaign of Italy (and why he failed), and his expedition to Egypt in 1798, his rise to power, and second campaign of Italy in 1799, and how he became the Emperor of France in 1804. We'll also be talking a bit about his personal life, what happened in Moscow, why he lost the Battle of Waterloo, and his exile (and eventual death) on the island of Saint Helena.

Without further ado, let's get started!

CHAPTER 1

Napoleon Bonaparte's Early Years

When it comes to Napoleon Bonaparte's early years, there's still quite a lot of controversy surrounding his birth and origins. Born in Ajaccio, Corsica, on August 15, 1769, Napoleon's life has been romanticized and debated in several different ways throughout history. Archbishop Whateley even humorously questioned whether Napoleon ever existed or if he was merely a name attributed to the French people collectively (McLynn, 2002). Psychologist Carl Gustav Jung suggested that Napoleon's significance was more collective than individual. In a way, he represented the resurgence of suppressed forces in the French psyche (McLynn, 2002).

The details of his birth and ancestry have been widely debated, which makes sense. After all, Napoleon Bonaparte was born a very long time ago. Some questioned whether he was truly Corsican; while others suggested that he had various exotic (and frankly unlikely) lineages — such as Greek, Carthaginian, or Moorish descent (McLynn, 2002). The speculations about his ancestry reveal just how complex Corsican history is. The Corsican influences that Napoleon grew up around probably played a major role in shaping who he turned out to be.

Napoleon was born to Carlo Bonaparte, a law student, and Marie-Letizia Ramolino. Both were descended from Italian mercenaries who settled in Corsica in the 16th century (McLynn, 2002). While some romanticized their marriage as a love match, it was more likely a dynastic alliance. Carlo's reluctance to marry in the Church and the objections of some Ramolino clan members certainly made their marriage a complicated one at the time.

Marie-Letizia's family had a military tradition, and her father served as an army officer with expertise in civil engineering. This contrasted with Carlo's family, who had a background in law (McLynn, 2002). It's widely believed that Napoleon was born into extreme poverty, but actually, his parents' property and income were relatively comfortable for the time.

It's worth mentioning that Napoleon was born during a rather turbulent time in Corsica. At the time, the island was experiencing a great deal of political turmoil (McLynn, 2002). For example, Corsica's struggle for independence (led by Pasquale Paoli) was a significant part of the island's history. Corsica's small population and unique political climate attracted admirers like Jean-Jacques Rousseau and James Boswell. Despite this, the French ultimately took control of Corsica in 1768, which led to the Bonaparte family fleeing into the mountains and Napoleon's birth during this period (McLynn, 2002).

Napoleon essentially grew up surrounded by these dramatic political events. There are no doubt that Corsica's stories of resistance, defeat, and betrayal shaped his early perspectives and conversations with others. Despite his later denial of Corsican significance, the island's history and politics left a lasting imprint on his mind.

It's fascinating to consider how growing up in Corsica impacted his leadership style when he eventually became the Emperor of France. His early experiences played a rather significant role in shaping the ambitious and formidable leader he would become. Let's break down the events of Napoleon Bonaparte's early life below.

Early Life and Education

Napoleon Bonaparte's early life was far from easy. His childhood is typically characterized by his family's (relatively) humble beginnings and their climb up the social ladder. Born in Corsica in 1769, he was one of twelve children, with only eight surviving infancy. This large family, including Napoleon's siblings (Joseph, Lucien, Elisa, Louis, Pauline, Caroline, and Jerome) had to navigate a challenging and ever-changing social and political landscape in Corsica (*1769-1793: Napoleon Bonaparte's Early Years - napoleon.org*, n.d.). As you may have guessed, Napoleon's early life and education laid the foundation for his future as a military leader (and, eventually, as the Emperor of France). Let's talk a bit more about the experiences and events that set him on the path to greatness, shall we?

NOBLE STATUS

In 1771, the Bonaparte family's noble status was officially recognized, which allowed young Napoleon to pursue his education at a prestigious military secondary school or "collège" in Brienne (*1769-1793: Napoleon Bonaparte's Early Years - napoleon.org*, n.d.). The recognition of his noble status was a significant development, as four degrees of nobility were required to gain entry into such an institution. Napoleon's father, Carlo Bonaparte, was eventually elected to be the Corsican Estates General (*1769-1793: Napoleon Bonaparte's Early Years - napoleon.org*, n.d.). He represented the nobility in the province of Ajaccio during several different periods in the 1770s.

EARLY EDUCATION

Napoleon's formal education began in 1774, at the age of five, when he enrolled in a primary boarding school in Ajaccio — which was run by Beguine lay sisters. He attended this school as a "day-boy" (if you're unfamiliar with this term, it refers to a male boarding student who both lives and studies at his boarding school). This was where Napoleon received his initial education. Two years later, his education took a more formal turn — he started studying French under Abbé

Recco, who happened to be a major influence on him *(1769-1793: Napoleon Bonaparte's Early Years - napoleon.org, n.d.).*

On December 16, 1778, Napoleon's life changed pretty significantly. His father and two older siblings traveled to mainland France. Meanwhile, Napoleon and his brother, Joseph, attended school in Autun on January 1, 1779, intending to improve their French language skills weighing heavily on both of their minds *(1769-1793: Napoleon Bonaparte's Early Years - napoleon.org, n.d.).* The decision to perfect his French was partly a decision that his father made for him, but Napoleon grew to understand just how important learning the language would be when it came to accessing greater opportunities in education (and society, in general).

MILITARY SCHOOL

Napoleon didn't end up staying in Autun for long, though. He spent three weeks with M. de Champeaux before being shipped off to the Royal Military Secondary School at Brienne-le-Château (1769-1793: Napoleon Bonaparte's Early Years - napoleon.org, n.d.). He was assigned to the "septième" class, which roughly translates to "seventh grade" in modern terms — although there's no direct modern equivalent. He held the status of an "élève pensionnaire du roi." This meant that he was a "king's scholar" (1769-1793: Napoleon Bonaparte's Early Years - napoleon.org, n.d.). Napoleon especially excelled at history and math (Napoleon's Rise & Fall: Illustrated Timeline – Virginia Museum of Fine Arts |, n.d.). This makes sense since Napoleon later became an artillery officer. You sort of have to be good at math to succeed in that particular military branch.

Despite doing quite well academically, Napoleon struggled during his time in military school. He was frequently teased by his classmates, which left him feeling isolated and distant a lot of the time (Chevalier, 2009). These first few years at Brienne posed many difficulties for young Napoleon, as he didn't quite fit in with the others. This very likely shaped his character and fueled his determination to prove himself.

Although he faced several challenges, Napoleon was finally able to embrace French culture while at Brienne. As stated before, he developed a keen interest in math, specifically algebra and geometry. His curiosity extended to geography and history, and he had a particular passion for the writings of Plutarch (Chevalier, 2009). This environment no doubt helped to sow the seeds for his future military career (which I'll be delving into in a bit). After completing his exams, and with a strong commitment to his military goals, Napoleon was able to secure a spot at the prestigious military school in Paris (Chevalier, 2009). Needless to say, this was a huge milestone for Napoleon. It's likely what set him on the path to being a successful artillery officer later on.

Recognizing Napoleon Bonaparte's impact on French history, Emperor Napoleon III decided to honor his legacy even further. In 1853, he granted the town of Brienne 400,000 francs, with 25,000 being put aside for a statue to be made in Napoleon Bonaparte's honor (Chevalier, 2009). The sculptor, Louis Rochet, was entrusted with building this statue. The statue portrays a young Napoleon in his school uniform, holding a copy of Plutarch's "Parallel Lives" in his left hand, with his right hand placed within his vest. Perhaps you've seen Napoleon Bonaparte striking this iconic pose in various films and works of art. Now you know where it comes from!

Napoleon Bonaparte's Early Military Career

In 1784, after completing his education at Brienne-le-Château, Napoleon enrolled at the prestigious École Militaire in Paris when he was just fifteen years old. Here, he would specialize as an artillery officer. While at École Militaire, he not only continued to excel in mathematics but also displayed a natural aptitude for leadership

(Knighton, 2017). It was clear, even at such a young age, that he was destined for great things.

Napoleon also spent a lot of time reading about the lives of historical leaders like Julius Caesar and Alexander the Great (Knighton, 2017). He meticulously studied their achievements and military strategies, which no doubt fueled his ambitions and helped to shape his future aspirations for leadership and power.

Artillery Officer

Napoleon's graduation from École Militaire in January 1786 marked the beginning of his early military career. He proudly served as a second lieutenant in an artillery regiment. However, his first assignments were less fulfilling than he hoped they would be. Stationed on garrison duty in provincial towns, he yearned for more meaningful and challenging opportunities (Knighton, 2017). During this period, he took a leave of absence to return to Corsica (which makes sense, seeing as he didn't have much to do at the time). Shortly before he returned to Corsica, his father became ill and died in 1785, which might further explain why Napoleon decided to take a leave of absence in 1786 (*Napoleon Bonaparte | eHISTORY*, n.d.).

The French Revolution that happened in 1789 favored Napoleon; it was his time to shine. He assumed leadership of a volunteer regiment in the complicated struggle between revolutionaries, conservatives, and Corsican nationalists on his home island. Much like his father, Napoleon initially aligned himself with Pasquale Paoli, who had returned to Corsica to lead the Nationalists in a civil war.

However, despite their shared values, Napoleon and Pasquale found themselves at odds on several different issues. The most contentious of these disagreements revolved around the accusation that Napoleon and his family were pro-French — a stance that incurred the wrath of the Nationalists who viewed them as opposed to

Corsican independence from France (*Napoleon Bonaparte | eHISTORY*, n.d.).

As tensions escalated, Napoleon eventually withdrew his support from the Nationalists, deciding to relocate his family to France in 1793 (*Napoleon Bonaparte | eHISTORY*, n.d.). Upon his return to France, Napoleon's presence played a major role in the revival of the French military. He wasted no time and swiftly rejoined his military unit in the city of Nice in June 1793. In doing so, he not only recommitted himself to the military but also threw his political support behind the Jacobins, a prominent political faction during the tumultuous times of the French Revolution.

The Jacobins were especially known for their progressive ideals and had gained significant popularity in the wake of the French Revolution. Their ascendancy to power was a brief but intense period, most commonly known as the "Reign of Terror," and it created a notable shift towards authoritarian rule (*Napoleon Bonaparte | eHISTORY*, n.d.). It's interesting to consider *why* exactly Napoleon decided to align himself with revolutionary Jacobinism. Perhaps he felt the need to align himself more with those who were in power.

THE SIEGE OF TOULON

In July 1793, Napoleon served as a captain in the regular army (Knighton, 2017). Toulon, a French naval stronghold and arsenal, became a center of royalist counterrevolutionary activities during this time. Negotiations unfolded between these royalists and British Vice Admiral Lord Hood, leading to a pact wherein they'd surrender the city to the British, provided they safeguarded Toulon and its ships for the captive young king, Louis XVII (The Editors of Encyclopaedia Britannica, 2023). Their goal was to reinstate the Constitution of 1791. This collaboration between the royalists and the British made things quite challenging for the French. It essentially carried the weight of the

Revolution's reputation, which made the recapture of Toulon not only important but necessary.

In early September, General Jean François Carteaux commenced the siege of Toulon. Initial efforts lacked fervor, though, and the situation persisted through the following month. However, when the French artillery commander in Toulon was injured, Napoleon was appointed to this position. It helped that he had a connection with Antoine Saliceti, a Corsican Montagnard deputy (The Editors of Encyclopaedia Britannica, 2023). Soon after, Napoleon earned a promotion to the rank of major, followed by adjutant general. The arrival of Spanish and English troops bolstered the city's defenses, which made matters even more complicated and intense.

About a month later, General Jacques Dugommier took charge, replacing Carteaux. Dugommier recognized Napoleon's potential and the two forged a strategic alliance to expel the British and their allies (The Editors of Encyclopaedia Britannica, 2023). Tensions escalated as British General Charles O'Hara arrived with reinforcements from Gibraltar. On November 30th, the garrison launched a surprise attack, routing French artillery units. An unforeseen encounter with Napoleon's forces followed, which resulted in O'Hara's capture (The Editors of Encyclopaedia Britannica, 2023).

The climax of the siege of Toulon came with a meticulously executed assault on the forts controlling the city's anchorage during the night of December 16-17 (The Editors of Encyclopaedia Britannica, 2023). Despite suffering a bayonet wound to his thigh while attacking Fort Mulgrave, Napoleon remained resolute on the battlefield. By December 18, French artillery under Napoleon's command opened fire on the British fleet, effectively neutralizing the city's defenses (The Editors of Encyclopaedia Britannica, 2023).

When Revolutionary forces regained control of the city on December 19, they imposed stern reprisals on the populace. Jacobins who had greeted the advancing troops faced brutal suppression, and violent acts continued even as Napoleon recuperated from his thigh injury. The aftermath witnessed the Revolutionary government's ruthless measures, including renaming the city Port-de-la-Montagne and leveling civilian buildings to their foundations (The Editors of Encyclopaedia Britannica, 2023).

Thousands faced execution or the guillotine as special tribunals, led by figures like Paul-François-Jean-Nicolas, Vicomte de Barras, Louis Fréron, and Augustin de Robespierre, enforced the government's retribution (The Editors of Encyclopaedia Britannica, 2023). On December 22, Napoleon was promoted to brigadier general at the age of twenty-four in a well-deserved recognition of the role he played in the capture of Toulon.

Following his triumph at Toulon, Napoleon emerged as one of the favored officers of the revolutionary government. He did, however, fall out of favor with Jacobin leadership, and narrowly avoided execution (*Napoleon Bonaparte | eHISTORY*, n.d.). Napoleon's achievements on the battlefield in Toulon propelled him forward, eventually earning him the position of commander of the Army of the Interior (*Napoleon Bonaparte | eHISTORY*, n.d.). He also gained recognition as a trusted military consultant for the French government. This set the stage for his rapid ascent through the military ranks — which I'll be diving into in the next chapter.

Chapter Summary

- August 15, 1769 — Napoleon was born in Ajaccio, Corsica. His parents were Carlo Bonaparte, and Marie-Letizia Ramolino.
- 1771 — The Bonaparte family's noble status was officially recognized.
- 1774 — Napoleon attended a Primary school run by the Beguine sisters.

- December 16, 1778 — His father and two older siblings traveled to mainland France.
- January 1, 1779 — Napoleon and his brother, Joseph, attended school in Autun. Three weeks later, he attended Royal Military Secondary School at Brienne-le-Château.
- 1784 — Napoleon completed his education at Brienne-le-Château and enrolled in École Militaire in Paris.
- January 1786 — Napoleon graduated from École Militaire and enrolled as a second lieutenant in an artillery regiment.
- 1785 — His father became ill and died.
- 1786 — Napoleon took a leave of absence.
- 1789 — The French Revolution started.
- 1793 — Napoleon relocated his family to France.
- June 1793 — Napoleon rejoined his military unit in the city of Nice.
- July 1793 — Napoleon led the artillery forces at the Siege of Toulon. He was promoted to brigadier general at the age of 24.

Segue

Even the most seasoned of history buffs don't know all that much about Napoleon's early life. The fact that he excelled in school and found his confidence on the battlefield says a lot about how he progressed through his military career and eventually became the Emperor of France. In the next chapter, I'll be talking about one of Napoleon's most famous (and, perhaps most heart-wrenching) failures: his Premiere campaign of Italy in 1796. This event served as a turning point for Napoleon, and despite ultimately failing, his determination never wavered. Let's get into it!

CHAPTER 2

Napoleon Bonaparte's Premiere Campaign of Italy

The Italian campaign of 1796-1797, led by the young and ambitious Napoleon Bonaparte, is one of the most notable parts of the French Revolutionary Wars (1792-1802). This campaign didn't just change how wars were fought but also had a major impact on European history in general. Napoleon's campaign ended with a significant defeat of Austria, ultimately putting northern Italy under French control and finally bringing an end to the long conflict (Mark, 2023). This campaign skyrocketed Napoleon Bonaparte to an unprecedented level of fame and power, although he also experienced the first real defeat of his career during this time (which I'll be talking more about shortly). Napoleon's Italian campaign reshaped the political landscape of Europe as people back then knew it (and, very likely, as we know it now).

When the First Coalition War (i.e. the first conflict of the Revolutionary Wars) began in 1792, most of the fighting was happening in places like Flanders and Germany. The Italian front was not the main stage. In March 1796, Napoleon took command of the Army of Italy. While doing this, he had no idea he would turn the Italian front into the most important part of the entire war (Mark, 2023). His daring and clever tactics amazed Europe as he consistently outsmarted and defeated every Austrian army sent his way.

Napoleon's unique strategies and brilliant way of thinking became evident as he swiftly moved through the Italian peninsula. He had a special talent for inspiring his troops, bringing together his diverse forces, and using surprise to gain an advantage during battles. The most significant battles of the Italian campaign — like Lodi, Arcole, and Rivoli — served as chances for him to show his tactical skills and, once again, left a lasting mark on European history. These victories not only established French dominance in northern Italy but also pushed Austria to seek a truce in October 1797, finally ending the long war (Mark, 2023).

The impact of Napoleon's Italian campaign reached far beyond just gaining new territory, though. This campaign very likely solidified his reputation as an outstanding military leader (Mark, 2023). His rapid rise to fame was so profound that he became one of the most influential figures in France (and all of Europe, for that matter). Let's talk about what exactly happened during Napoleon's Italian campaign below so that you can gain a deeper understanding of his successes as well as his failures during this period of his life.

Napoleon Takes Command of the French Army of Italy

On March 27th, 1796, General Napoleon Bonaparte arrived in the picturesque town of Nice to take on an important assignment. It had been a whirlwind month for the young general, who was a mere twenty-six years old at the time and had received his command just seven days before marrying Josephine de Beauharnais. Josephine was previously the mistress of Paul Barras — a prominent figure within the French Directory and one of the most influential men in France. This led to rumors suggesting that Bonaparte's appointment was merely a favor granted to him by Barras in consideration of his prior involvement with Josephine (Mark, 2023). Nevertheless, Napoleon had already earned a reputation in the French army, having distinguished himself during the Siege of Toulon in 1793.

Upon his arrival in Nice, Napoleon immediately set out to inspect the troops under his command. What he encountered was a demoralized, ragged force teetering on the brink of mutiny. The soldiers were starving and malnourished, having received meager rations at exorbitant prices from corrupt contractors. Basic supplies like muskets, bayonets, and uniforms were in short supply, and some battalions lacked appropriate footwear. The army had gone unpaid for months, and when the payment finally arrived, it came in the form of nearly worthless banknotes known as "mandats territoriaux," which was all that the virtually bankrupt French Directory could offer (Mark, 2023). The ravages of disease, desertion, and battlefield losses had reduced the army from its initial strength of 106,000 men in 1792 to a mere 37,600 men and 60 guns by March 1796, with no prospects of reinforcements in sight (Mark, 2023). Napoleon faced the monumental task of restoring order and efficiency to this woefully depleted force.

The French troops had to feed themselves off of the sustenance of the countryside and protect their exposed coastline against potential British and Sardinian naval raids. Shortly after arriving, Napoleon relocated the army's headquarters — shifting it about forty-two miles forward from Nice to Albenga. On March 28th, he wrote to the Directory: "Administrative situation of the army is bad, but no longer desperate…. From now on, the army will eat good bread and will have meat, and it has already had considerable advances on its back pay…. I shall march in a short while" (Lombardy, 2013).

Napoleon also familiarized himself with his fellow officers, many of whom would go on to play important roles in the history of the Napoleonic era. His chief of staff, Alexandre Berthier, was an administrative virtuoso capable of maintaining a grueling 20-hour workday and keeping pace with Napoleon's rapid and occasionally brutal commands (Mark, 2023). The division commanders included Jean Sérurier, a veteran general with thirty-four years of experience in the former Royal Army; Pierre Augereau, a former mercenary and duelist, who had once taken a life over an insult; and André Masséna, a talented general whose voracious appetite for both loot and romance was legendary. Among the officers who would later achieve great renown under Napoleon's command were Joachim Murat, Jean-Andoche Junot, Jean Lannes, Barthélemy Joubert, and Auguste Marmont (Mark, 2023).

Initially, these officers had doubts about their newly appointed commander-in-chief. At just twenty-six years old, the diminutive and wiry Napoleon hardly resembled the image of a seasoned general. His proud display of his wife's portrait struck many as juvenile and frivolous. However, they would soon discover just how great of a leader Napoleon was. Napoleon immediately initiated a reorganization of the army's supply chain. He took on venal contractors and confronted the corruption that had plagued the ranks. He also called back the cavalry from their winter quarters and secured a loan of three million francs from Genoese financiers (Mark, 2023). He was quickly able to reinstate discipline by disbanding mutinous battalions and court-martialing two officers for singing anti-revolutionary songs. Within a matter of days, Napoleon had gained the respect and admiration of his subordinates (Mark, 2023).

His next challenge was to win the loyalty and support of the rank-and-file soldiers. He pledged to them the promise of glory and wealth — rewards that had previously been afforded only to their compatriots in Germany and Flanders. This was a bold promise, especially considering that Napoleon had yet to lead an army into actual battle. On the 10th of April, just five days before he intended to launch his campaign, he received word that a formidable force of fifty-three thousand Austrian and Piedmontese troops was already advancing towards him (Mark, 2023). The moment had arrived for Napoleon to confront his destiny on the battlefield.

Napoleon's First Victories as Commander-in-Chief

Since 1793, the Kingdom of Piedmont-Sardinia had conflicted with the French Republic. However, as time passed, their commitment to the battle began to fall by the wayside. A thick cloud of suspicion hung over the relationship between the Piedmontese and their Austrian allies, with each side doubting the other's intentions. Even the Austrian commander, Johan Beaulieu, had received advice against placing excessive trust in the Piedmontese (Mark, 2023). In response to this situation, Napoleon devised a clever strategy to create a divide between the two opposing armies and defeat them individually.

On the 12th of April, Napoleon executed his plan. He launched an attack on Montenotte — a mountain village where the enemy's defensive line was stretched dangerously thin. Under the guidance of André Masséna, one of Napoleon's capable division commanders, the French forces executed a skillful maneuver. They encircled the exposed right flank of the enemy during heavy rainfall. In the aftermath, the coalition of Austrians and Piedmontese suffered heavy losses, with two-thousand-five-hundreds of their soldiers falling, while the French only incurred 800 casualties (Mark, 2023).

In the days that followed, Napoleon secured two more decisive victories at Millesimo on the 13th of April and Dego on the 14th of April, respectively (Mark, 2023). These triumphs allowed him to effectively drive a wedge between the retreating Piedmontese and Austrian armies. With his adversaries now separated, Napoleon was able to initiate an invasion of Piedmont. A week later, at the Battle of Mondovì on the 21st of April, he inflicted another substantial blow on the Piedmontese, effectively opening the path to their capital city, Turin (Mark, 2023). Faced with this relentless assault, the Kingdom of Piedmont-Sardinia had no alternative but to beg for peace. On the 28th of April, they agreed to the Armistice of Cherasco, which served as the end of these hostilities (Mark, 2023). In under a month of campaigning, Napoleon had successfully neutralized one of his adversaries. Now, he would have to deal with the Austrian forces.

The Battle of Lodi

Napoleon Bonaparte was a shrewd tactician and master of deception. His campaign in Italy showed just how brilliant he was. Consider his ingenious use of a 'secret' clause in the Treaty of Cherasco, for example, which granted him access to the bridge at Valenza over the River Po (Mark, 2023). When this information was inadvertently leaked to the vigilant Austrian General Beaulieu, who guarded the pass, it seemed like a misstep on Napoleon's part. However, this apparent error was a cunning ruse. Napoleon had secretly planned to cross the River Po at Piacenza, to the east of Valenza (Mark, 2023). This caught the Austrians off guard, which forced them to withdraw so that they could protect the road to Milan.

The French forces pursued the Austrians, which ultimately led to the Battle of Lodi on the 10th of May. When the French arrived at the scene, most of the Austrian army had already crossed the Adda River, leaving only a rearguard force behind in the town of Lodi. This rearguard was pushed back, at first, by the determined grenadiers under General Lannes. However, Napoleon was determined to capture the bridge across the Adda before the Austrians could destroy it (Mark, 2023). This wasn't going to be easy, so carabiniers under Colonel Dupas valiantly accepted the perilous duty of leading the assault. The momentous charge onto the bridge took place at 5 p.m., amidst a relentless hail of Austrian grapeshot (This was a cannon charge that was typically made up of small round lead or iron projectiles. It was usually used as an anti-personnel weapon. Grapeshots were typically arranged in clusters of three iron rings, and these small iron balls were organized in three tiers using cast-iron plates and a central connecting rod). Undeterred, the French soldiers courageously waded into the river's shallows, firing at the Austrian gunners positioned on the opposite side. Wave after wave of French assaults finally secured the bridge — another victory for Napoleon Bonaparte (Mark, 2023).

The Battle of Lodi might not seem all that significant in the grand scheme of things. Both sides suffered similar casualties, and the Austrians were already in retreat by this point. However, this particular battle revealed the bravery of the French soldiers as well as Napoleon's military finesse. His triumph at Lodi not only earned him the admiration of his men, but they also bestowed upon him the affectionate nickname of "the Little Corporal" (Mark, 2023). This battle also solidified Napoleon's belief in his destiny to be a great leader.

Despite the resounding success at Lodi and his growing popularity, Napoleon faced a subtle challenge from the Directory in Paris during this time. The Directory proposed a plan that would have seen him share command of the Army of Italy with the more experienced General Kellermann of the Army of the Alps, which would potentially dilute Napoleon's authority (Mark, 2023). Napoleon staunchly refused to divide his command, even going to the extent of threatening resignation should such an arrangement be forced upon him. The Directory quickly abandoned the scheme, which allowed Napoleon to continue his relentless pursuit of greatness on the battlefield.

The Army of Italy Enters Milan

On the 15th of May 1796, Milan witnessed a momentous occasion as Napoleon Bonaparte's Army of Italy made its triumphant entry into the city (Mark, 2023). The people of Milan greeted their liberators with understandable enthusiasm — their hearts no doubt brimming with relief (since they no longer had to deal with the Austrian army). Napoleon wasted no time in setting his ambitious plans into motion. It was truly the inception of a new era — not only for Milan but for the entire region. His immediate goal was to revamp the governance of Milan, as this would pave the way for the creation of a 'sister republic,' which would essentially become a French satellite state known as the Transpadane Republic (Mark, 2023).

Under Napoleon's guidance, a new constitution was crafted, which would serve as the basic framework for this new republic. He appointed Italian Jacobins to important governmental positions — a strategy that was meant to help grow a strong network of pro-French political clubs that would lend their support to the nascent order (Mark, 2023). Although this transformation was presented as a liberating force, it concealed the pragmatic need to secure funding for the Army of Italy.

Napoleon requisitioned around twenty million francs from Milan, as well as from the dukes of Parma and Modena. This was the first time that the army had been paid in cash since 1793 (Mark, 2023). This was a big win for the Army of Italy but it was evident that Napoleon wanted more. As the victor of Milan, Napoleon was able to afford his generals the ability to exploit their authority. The city, after all, was a treasure trove of wealth and priceless artworks; and the French officers did not hesitate to lay their hands on these treasures, eventually shipping them back to Paris (Mark, 2023).

On the 21st of May, Napoleon traveled to Mantua, where the Austrian General Beaulieu had sought refuge with his retreating army. However, he had scarcely left Milan when reports of uprisings breaking out in Milan and Pavia reached him (Mark, 2023). He quickly traveled back to Milan with a determination to quell the insurrections, and, once again, assert the authority of the Transpadane Republic.

In the face of these uprisings, Napoleon gave out stern retribution to the Italian rebels. He laid siege to Pavia, and upon its capture, he allowed his troops to engage in unbridled plunder for several hours (Mark, 2023). Meanwhile, General Lannes — another one of Napoleon's trusted commanders — was dispatched to deal with the rebellious town of Binasco. He swiftly executed all of the men living there, leaving the town in ashes (Mark, 2023). These brutal measures were intended to serve as a warning to the rest of occupied Italy. It was a grim reminder of the steep price to be paid for defying their French "liberators."

Napoleon Besieges Mantua

Mantua — strategically positioned within the Quadrilateral — was essentially a network of four fortresses guarding the Alpine passes. It was the key to Austrian dominance in northern Italy at the time (Mark, 2023). When Napoleon initiated the siege of Mantua on the 2nd of June — as usual, leading a well-reinforced and supplied army — it became extremely important for the Austrians to prevent Napoleon and his army from capturing the city.

Field Marshal Dagobert von Wurmser, a veteran of the Seven Years' War, was entrusted with the command of fifty-thousand troops and tasked to relieve the besieged city at any cost (Mark, 2023). Recognizing the urgency of the situation, Wurmser came up with a strategic plan to expedite his forces. He decided to divide his army, with eighteen-thousand troops led by General Quasdanovich advancing down the west side of Lake Garda, while Wurmser himself took control of the remaining thirty-two-thousand troops, progressing down the east side (Mark, 2023). Napoleon realized that he was going to have to defeat each of these armies — one at a time — before they could successfully unite.

At the end of July, Napoleon decided to temporarily lift the siege of Mantua. During this hiatus, he left behind one hundred-and-seventy-nine cannons and mortars, disposing of their ammunition in the nearby lakes. In two days — from the 3rd to the 4th of August — he somehow managed to vanquish General Quasdanovich at the Second Battle of Lonato (Mark, 2023).

He then confronted Wurmser's forces at the Battle of Castiglione, once again emerging victorious the very next day. These hard-fought battles took a toll, of course. They resulted in a loss of approximately five-thousand men on both sides (Mark, 2023). However, the outcome ultimately forced the retreating Austrians to abandon their goal of relieving Mantua and provided Napoleon with the opportunity to recommence the siege.

Remarkably undeterred, Wurmser regrouped and initiated another offensive toward the end of August. A series of confrontations unfolded between Napoleon and Wurmser during this time, all of which eventually culminated in the Battle of Bassano on the 8th of September (Mark, 2023). Faced with another defeat, Wurmser was forced to retreat toward Mantua.

Unfortunately, his ill-fated attempt to provide relief for the city only exacerbated the plight of the garrison within. With the addition of Wurmser's troops, the available provisions were insufficient to sustain the entire besieged population (Mark, 2023). As desperation loomed, the Austrians resorted to consuming horseflesh, and in a cruel twist of fate, disease and malnutrition began to claim the lives of one-hundred-and-fifty soldiers and civilians each day. Even amidst such dire suffering, Wurmser remained resolute. It was quite a brutal situation, and the protracted siege of Mantua bore witness to the determination displayed by both the besieging and besieged forces in the end (Mark, 2023).

Defeat at the Second Battle of Bassano

In November 1796, Napoleon faced what was, perhaps, one of the most harrowing challenges of his early military career. Few people know what happened at the Second Battle of Bassano but I'm here to provide the truth, so listen closely. Napoleon's opponent, this time, was the sixty-one-year-old Hungarian General József Alvinczi — who would later earn Napoleon's respect as one of his toughest adversaries during his Italian campaign (Mark, 2023). Alvinczi led the Austrian forces in their third attempt to break the siege. On November 2nd,

Alvinczi ordered his troops to cross the Piave River, while General Quasdanovich's forces advanced toward Vicenza via Bassano.

Napoleon tried to stop Quasdanovich's advance but he quickly found himself outnumbered and overwhelmed. He had no choice but to withdraw — the first real defeat of his military career (Mark, 2023). Falling back to Vicenza, Napoleon received news of a French division under General Vaubois suffering a devastating loss near Cembra and Calliano. In response, he took action to restore discipline, relieving Vaubois of his command and giving a stern message to his troops: "Soldiers of the 39th and 85th Infantry, you no longer meet the standards of the French Army... your flags will bear the inscription, 'these men are no longer part of the Army of Italy" (Mark, 2023). Surprisingly, this public reprimand motivated the demibrigades, and they fought with determination in the battles to come.

Napoleon's Italian campaign reached its lowest point on November 12th when his forces defended Verona against a relentless Austrian assault. Both sides took a break on the following day, and the French army was basically in despair. Napoleon even wrote a letter to the Directory, acknowledging the grim circumstances: "Perhaps the hour... of my own death is near... we are abandoned in the depths of Italy" (Mark, 2023). Despite this, Napoleon refused to admit defeat. On November 15th, he initiated an attack on Alvinczi at the Battle of Arcole — with the most intense fighting happening around a bridge over the Adige River.

The battle on the bridge was grueling, and Napoleon's aide-de-camp tragically lost his life. Napoleon narrowly escaped his death when he was knocked off the bridge and into the mud below (Mark, 2023). Although it took two more days and resulted in three-thousand casualties, the French ultimately succeeded in capturing the bridge. Talk about bringing yourself back from the brink of disaster!

The Fall of Mantua

Napoleon's relentless Italian campaign continued, with his sights firmly set on the city of Mantua. This city had become somewhat of a bastion for the Austrians, as it housed eighteen-thousand-five-hundred soldiers (although only nine-thousand-eight-hundred remained fit for duty) (Mark, 2023). Within the walls of Mantua, the situation had grown quite bleak. Food supplies were dwindling and the Austrian army was understandably exhausted.

In a final attempt to relieve Mantua, General József Alvinczi led his forces into a confrontation with the French on January 14, 1797, at the Battle of Rivoli (Mark, 2023). The French were, once again, victorious. Although they suffered losses of three-thousand men, the Austrians had four-thousand casualties, in addition to eight-thousand taken as prisoners of war (Mark, 2023). The Battle of Rivoli essentially extinguished any chance of hope for Mantua, and the city had no choice but to surrender on February 2. By this point, around sixteen-thousand-three-hundred Austrian soldiers had succumbed to starvation and disease (Mark, 2023).

The fall of Mantua was a major victory for Napoleon during his Italian Campaign. Now that Mantua was under his control, his army would be able to pursue Vienna — which was Napoleon's main goal. On March 10, 1797, Napoleon led forty-thousand troops through Tyrol, advancing towards Klagenfurt and eventually reaching Loeben in Styria (Mark, 2023). While he had a few "scuffs" here and there with Archduke Charles, the brother of the Austrian emperor, the Austrians were cautious about risking another full-blown battle with the French. They still faced threats from French forces along the Rhine. For this reason, they pursued an armistice, which Napoleon accepted on April 2 at Loeben (Mark, 2023). The terms of this armistice were later formalized on October 17, 1797, with the signing of the Treaty of Campo Formio.

Napoleon played a major role in these negotiations. He even negotiated on behalf of the French Republic without consulting the Directory beforehand (Mark, 2023). Through these negotiations, he eventually got Austria to acknowledge French control over Belgium, and the left bank of the Rhine. He also established a new sister republic in Italy — known as the Cisalpine Republic. In exchange for Austria's territorial concessions, Napoleon offered them territories belonging to the neutral Serene Republic of Venice. Venice was then partitioned between Austria and the Cisalpine Republic, effectively concluding the Serene Republic's one-thousand-two-hundred-year history (Mark, 2023). It's all too clear that Napoleon's diplomatic finesse (as well as his many military victories) reshaped the political landscape of Europe.

Chapter Summary

- 1792 — The First Coalition War began.
- March 1796 — Napoleon took command of the Army of Italy.
- April 12, 1796 — Napoleon launched an attack on Montenotte. In the aftermath, the coalition of Austrians and Piedmontese suffered heavy losses.
- April 13 and 14, 1796 — Napoleon secured two more victories at Millesimo. A week later, at the Battle of Mondovì on April 21st, he inflicted another substantial blow on the Piedmontese, effectively opening the path to their capital city, Turin.
- May 10, 1796 — Napoleon secured another victory at the Battle of Lodi. This battle solidified Napoleon's belief in his destiny to be a great leader
- May 15, 1796 — Napoleon's army entered Milan. Uprisings broke out in Milan after he left for Mantua on May 21st. General Lannes, Napoleon's trusted commander, was dispatched to deal with the rebellious town of Binasco. He

- executed all of the men living there — a brutal measure that was intended to serve as a warning to the rest of occupied Italy.
- June 2nd, 1796 — When Napoleon initiated the siege of Mantua.
- November 1796 — Napoleon experienced defeat at the second battle of Bassano.
- January 14, 1797 — In a final attempt to relieve Mantua, General József Alvinczi led his forces into a confrontation with the French. The city surrendered on February 2nd.
- March 10, 1797 — Napoleon led forty-thousand troops through Tyrol, advancing towards Klagenfurt and eventually reaching Loeben in Styria.
- October 17, 1797 — The terms of an armistice were formalized with the signing of the Treaty of Campo Formio.

Segue

Napoleon's Italian campaign during 1796 and 1797 was the dawn of a new era. Many historians (including myself) believe that it played an important role in France's success during the French Revolutionary Wars. His Italian campaign is probably also what gave Napoleon the confidence he needed to rise through the ranks and eventually become Emperor of France. Despite being only twenty-eight years old by this point, Napoleon could say that he had dramatically altered the map of northern Italy, breathed life into new republics, and humbled one of Europe's major powers. Would you believe that this was just the beginning of Napoleon's story? In the next chapter, I'll be discussing his 1798 expedition to Egypt and what he accomplished there, so stick around!

CHAPTER 3

Napoleon Bonaparte's Expedition to Egypt

In April of 1798, Napoleon Bonaparte was entrusted with taking command of the newly formed Army of the Orient. This event kicked off France's expedition to Egypt. The intentions of France's post-revolutionary Directory behind this endeavor were twofold. They not only wanted to disrupt Britain's trade route to India and rekindle commercial ties with the Levant, but they were also aiming to neutralize Napoleon (though, this was something no one would speak of out loud). His popularity following the triumphs of his Italian Campaign the year before posed a looming threat in the political landscape of the time.

Upon arriving in Egypt, Napoleon addressed his troops, stating: "From the heights of the Pyramids, forty centuries look down on us" (National Gallery of Victoria, n.d.). Yet, the experience of France's Egyptian Campaign didn't quite match up with the glory and splendor suggested by this statement. Surviving French officers vividly described the harrowing reality of Napoleon's decision to lead his thirty-seven-thousand troops across the arid desert, rather than following the safer path of the Nile River from Alexandria. Their accounts are filled with tales of abysmal mismanagement, desperate thirst, grueling discomfort, rampant disease, and tragic death (National Gallery of Victoria, n.d.). Perhaps Napoleon was attempting to test the mettle and endurance of his soldiers, but that's just speculation.

Amidst the seemingly insurmountable challenges and grueling conditions, something really important happened during the Battle of the Pyramids (more accurately known as the Battle of Embabeh in the Gaza Plain, where the battle took place). It was here that Napoleon, once again, showed his remarkable military acumen. He decided to employ the massive "divisional square" — a strategy rooted in antiquity but revitalized by his genius. This tactic would ultimately help the French secure victory over the legendary and seemingly invincible Mameluke cavalry, who had effectively ruled Egypt since the thirteenth century (National Gallery of Victoria, n.d.). Their fearless reputation was shattered as they faced defeat at the hands of Napoleon Bonaparte. In this section, we'll be talking about how, exactly, Napoleon accomplished this.

The Directory Approves Napoleon's Expedition to Egypt

In 1797, a significant shift in power dynamics occurred within the French Republic. France had achieved dominance in Western Europe, earning victories over most of its adversaries in the War of the First Coalition. Among France's few remaining opponents was Great Britain. Despite tentative overtures of peace in 1797, British Prime Minister William Pitt the Younger was determined to forge a second anti-French coalition. Of course, the French Directory was equally determined to bring the war to a definitive conclusion (Mark, 2023). Undeterred, they put together an army of one-hundred-and-twenty-thousand men, ready, at any time, to invade Britain. Tasked with leading this force was none other than Napoleon Bonaparte. Who, after all, could be better for the job?

Napoleon took a tour of the nation's dockyards to figure out just how feasible this expedition would be. Unfortunately, his assessment left him feeling rather disheartened. British naval supremacy rendered any prospective invasion a futile endeavor. In light of this obstacle, Napoleon proposed a different route to victory. He advocated for the

French Republic to establish a colony in Egypt — a concept that had been intermittently considered by French leadership since the 1760s (Mark, 2023).

The urgent need to counter Britain's might and regain the lost colonies in the West Indies made the prospect of Egypt particularly enticing to the Directory. Egypt's location made it an ideal base from which the French could challenge British interests — not only in the Mediterranean but also in the Indian subcontinent. Napoleon even considered forging alliances with anti-British factions in India, including Tipu Sultan (Mark, 2023). While the Directory had some reservations, they also recognized the potential benefits of such an expedition. At the very least, they would finally be able to rid themselves of the increasingly influential Napoleon, who, again, was seen as a threat because of his growing popularity.

Naturally, Napoleon's ambitions drove this broader geopolitical scheme, too. He wanted to emulate his hero, Alexander the Great, by establishing an eastern empire. Without hesitation, the Directory granted their approval for the expedition, contingent upon Napoleon personally securing the necessary funds and returning to France within six months. Napoleon was quickly able to procure the required eight million francs, obtaining so-called "contributions" from France's sister republics in Holland, Switzerland, and Italy. With meticulous precision, he handpicked twenty-one of the most elite demibrigades in France, eventually amassing a force of around thirty-eight-thousand soldiers (Mark, 2023). His officer corps included some of the most skilled generals within the French army, specifically Alexandre Berthier, Jean-Baptiste Kléber, Louis Desaix, Louis-Andre Bon, Jean Reynier, and Jacques Menou. Napoleon also enlisted the support of his stepson, Eugene de Beauharnais, and his brother, Louis, who served as aides-de-camp (Mark, 2023).

Not only that, but Napoleon enlisted the services of one-hundred-and-sixty-seven distinguished scientists and scholars from France.

Guided by the mathematician, Gaspard Monge, these scholars were given a mission to conduct research and display the advancements that European science had made at the time (Mark, 2023). Their presence would eventually bring about the discovery of the Rosetta Stone and signal the birth of modern Egyptology. Napoleon had more than just military conquest on his mind when he decided to go on his Egyptian expedition!

The British Naval Threat

Before setting their sights on Egypt, the French military made a stopover in Malta, where they successfully captured the island on June 12th, 1798 (*Egyptian Campaign*, n.d.). Their goal was to establish a French presence in Egypt, as this would disrupt British interests and potentially create a strategic base for operations in India. On July 1st, the French troops arrived in Egypt, and the very next day, they seized control of the coastal city of Alexandria (*Egyptian Campaign*, n.d.). With this seemingly effortless victory in their grasp, they were able to turn their attention toward the ultimate prize: the ancient city of Cairo.

Still, though, Napoleon's advance into Egypt was met with fierce resistance from the Mamaluke army. On July 21st, the two forces clashed in a historic confrontation known as the Battle of the Pyramids (*Egyptian Campaign*, n.d.). Faced with relentless mass cavalry charges, the French forces used the strategy of forming large squares to withstand the onslaught. This way, no one could attack the French soldiers from behind.

These "infantry squares" were frequently used by infantry units (as the name suggests) during combat. Infantry officers would form their units into squares (rather than straight lines), which made it much more difficult for groups of enemy soldiers to pull off successful attacks. Infantry squares are considered to be pretty old-fashioned nowadays since guns have gotten considerably more advanced. Forming infantry squares was a very smart move on Napoleon's part, and it allowed the French to, once again, emerge victorious. Napoleon, being a man who never wasted time, took control of Egypt and then moved his forces to occupy the city of Cairo on the following day.

Things were going well for the French, and Napoleon was no doubt pleased with himself. Despite his initial success, though, he would soon have to face a threat looming on the seas. The British, obviously alarmed by the prospect of Egypt falling under French dominion, devised a plan. They dispatched Rear-Admiral Horatio Nelson with a strong British fleet to intercept the advancing French expedition at sea (*Egyptian Campaign*, n.d.).

Although Nelson ultimately failed to impede Napoleon's progress in the Mediterranean, he did manage to achieve a decisive victory during the intense Battle of the Nile — a naval battle that raged from August 1st to 3rd in 1798 (*Egyptian Campaign*, n.d.). Once again, the British reigned supreme when it came to naval forces, so this wasn't a huge surprise. This British victory not only weakened the position of Napoleon and the French but also gave the Mamalukes and Ottomans the confidence they needed to continue their resistance against the French invasion (*Egyptian Campaign*, n.d.).

The French Occupy Cairo

With a substantial part of Egypt under his control, Napoleon Bonaparte wanted to gain the trust and favor of the local population. In the busy streets of Cairo, he actively engaged with the locals in spirited theological discussions, perhaps in an attempt to display to them his knowledge of the Quran (Mark, 2023). Even more intriguingly, Napoleon subtly hinted at the prospect of embracing Islam.

On August 20th, a celebration took place in honor of the Prophet Muhammad's birthday. During these three days of festivities, Napoleon was bestowed with the honorary title of "son-in-law of the Prophet" and the illustrious name "Ali-Bonaparte" (Mark, 2023). This helped to create a sense of camaraderie and promote the acceptance of the French presence within the city. On the last day of these festivities, Napoleon inaugurated the Institut d'Egypte. This institution, run by the mathematician, Gaspard Monge, was created to impress the people of Cairo with enlightenment ideals, scientific discoveries, and the spirit of reason (Mark, 2023).

Everything was going according to Napoleon's plan — or so he thought. Little did he know that discontent was simmering among the Egyptian people. In September, the grand promise made by Charles-Maurice de Talleyrand fell through as the Ottoman Empire declared war on France. By October 20th, news had reached Cairo that the Ottomans were putting together an army in Syria and were ready for an assault on Napoleon's forces (Mark, 2023). Things were getting pretty Chaotic in Cairo, at the time, too. The military governor, General Dupuy, died in the streets, and fifteen of Napoleon's bodyguards and one of his trusted aides-de-camp fell victim to the violent upheaval as well. Before Napoleon could come up with a response, three-hundred French soldiers had fallen, and the Cairene rebels had sought refuge within the sanctuary of the Gama-el-Azhar Grand Mosque (Mark, 2023).

Napoleon had no choice but to respond with an iron fist. He subjected the revered Grand Mosque to a relentless artillery bombardment, and then unleashed his infantry upon it, which led to the desecration of this sacred site (Mark, 2023). The confrontation ended up culminating in the demise of approximately two-thousand-five-hundred rebels, and over the following weeks, countless others were executed. Napoleon went so far as to sanction beheadings. He even piled up the heads in the middle of the city for all to see while the bodies were cast into the Nile (Mark, 2023). On November 11th, the insurrection had been successfully voided, which allowed Napoleon to redirect his attention towards the escalating threat in Syria.

Napoleon Campaigns in Syria

In February of 1799, Napoleon led thirteen-thousand men out of Egypt. He commanded four war-weary divisions under the leadership of generals Reynier, Kléber, Bon, and Jean Lannes, while the cavalry was overseen by Joachim Murat (Mark, 2023). On February 17th, Napoleon's advance was quickly stopped when he ran into an Ottoman garrison of two-thousand soldiers defending the El-Arish fortress.

Undeterred, as usual, he bombed the fortress, and just two days later, the defenders yielded — emerging from the fortress after solemnly swearing by the Quran not to take up arms against their conquerors once more (Mark, 2023). With El-Arish secured, the French forces continued their march, passing through Gaza before launching the Siege of Jaffa on March 3rd.

The siege lasted a mere three days before Napoleon dispatched a messenger bearing news that he planned to take over the city. The governor of Jaffa obviously wasn't happy about this, so he not only beheaded the messenger but shamelessly exhibited his severed head on one of the city's walls (Mark, 2023). The next day, hordes of infuriated French troops stormed the city. Napoleon allowed Jaffa to suffer through an entire day of looting and violence, simply for the sake of seeking revenge and establishing his dominance. His brutality didn't end there, though. Motivated by a malevolent desire for retribution against the Jaffa garrison — many of whom were the very soldiers he had previously released following the capture of El-Arish — Napoleon hatched a plan.

On March 9th, between two and three thousand prisoners of war were assembled on a beach south of Jaffa, where they were mercilessly slaughtered by Napoleon and his forces (Mark, 2023). Napoleon justified this ruthless act by claiming that there was a shortage of provisions to support the prisoners, despite his forces having recently acquired around four-hundred-thousand rations of biscuits in Jaffa

(Mark, 2023). Shortly after these horrors occurred in Jaffa, the French troops were infected with the bubonic plague.

Perhaps it was karma at work or simply a cruel twist of fate. With a mortality rate of nine-two-percent, new cases were detected at a rate of two-hundred-and-seventy daily (Mark, 2023). While Napoleon made every effort to tend to the afflicted and provide for his men, his stay in the plagued city could only be prolonged for so long. On March 14th, he assembled the able-bodied soldiers and set out on a fresh campaign towards Acre (Mark, 2023).

The Siege of Acre

On March 18, 1799, Napoleon's army arrived at the gates of Acre. Napoleon knew that Acre would be a challenge. The city was well-defended, under the command of Jezzar Pasha, who was known for his ruthless tactics. He was even nicknamed "the butcher" (Mark, 2023), which should tell you something. The Ottomans, aided by the British commodore Sir Sidney Smith — who used psychological warfare to unsettle the French, received plenty of supplies and reinforcements. Smith's strategies included preventing the besieging French forces from receiving any news from France. This, in turn, deepened their sense of isolation (Mark, 2023).

Napoleon was confident, at first, that he'd be able to capture Acre fairly quickly. However, his optimism quickly dwindled when an enemy flotilla captured his heavy siege artillery. The French found themselves facing their own captured cannons, which Napoleon was not prepared for. Consequently, he had to use slower, more conventional siege methods, like sapping, which involved digging trenches to approach the city walls (Mark, 2023).

Things started going downhill from there. On March 28th, Napoleon's attempt to storm the city failed due to French ladders being too short to scale the walls. Over the next nine weeks, Napoleon ordered eight more major attacks, all of which ended in defeat (Mark,

2023) The French siege encampment extended into mosquito-infested swampland, which led to a malaria outbreak among the troops. It was all-around disastrous, and as French casualties piled up, Napoleon also suffered the loss of several talented officers. General Cafferelli succumbed to gangrene on April 28th, and General Bon was mortally wounded on May 10th (Mark, 2023).

Despite all of this, the French army was able to score a victory against an Ottoman relief army at the Battle of Mount Tabor on April 16th. Still, though, this relatively small achievement did little to improve Napoleon's chances of capturing Acre. The situation worsened when Sir Sidney Smith allowed a piece of true news to reach the besieged French army — a newspaper report on the start of the War of the Second Coalition and France's military defeats in Europe. Napoleon reluctantly lifted the siege on May 20th. and began the arduous journey back to Cairo. The failure to conquer Acre haunted him. He would later say: "I missed my destiny at Acre" (Mark, 2023).

Napoleon Retreats

Upon arriving in Cairo on June 14th, 1799, Napoleon immediately took stock of his situation. Recognizing the precariousness of his position, he gathered every available soldier and set off towards Alexandria. When they reached their destination, a new challenge was waiting for them, however. Sir Sidney Smith had managed to transport fifteen-thousand Ottoman soldiers under the command of Mustapha Pasha to Aboukir (Mark, 2023). This set the stage for the Battle of Aboukir, which would ultimately result in Napoleon's last triumph in Egypt. The battle fought on July 25th, caused the deaths of around two-thousand Ottoman soldiers. The French, meanwhile, suffered less than one-thousand casualties (Mark, 2023). However, with the French fleet under Admiral Brueys obliterated, and France once again at war with its European neighbors, the reality of the situation was bleak — no reinforcements were coming.

Leaving behind a frustrated army in Egypt, Napoleon set sail on August 23rd with only a handful of officers and scholars. He left the rest of his men stranded in Alexandria, completely unaware of his intentions (Mark, 2023). Curiously, he abandoned his men, as not much of the French army remained, anyway (remember, there were no reinforcements left), but perhaps Napoleon simply panicked at the time and wanted to start with a clean slate in France. A little over a month later, he made his triumphant return to France, and before the year's end, he seized control of the French government in the Coup of 18 Brumaire.

Unsurprisingly, the soldiers and officers he left behind in Egypt felt betrayed by Napoleon's sudden departure and abandonment. Among the disgruntled was General Kléber, who harbored intense resentment for Napoleon. He vowed to get his revenge, mockingly referring to Napoleon as "that Corsican runt" (Mark, 2023). It's interesting that, even as a successful leader, Napoleon was seen as an outsider by his troops (though, they had every right to be upset with him after he abandoned them). Kléber's opportunity for retribution against Napoleon, however, never came to pass. In June of 1800, he was assassinated in Alexandria.

General Menou took control after that and became responsible for the defense of Alexandria. The city came under siege when an Anglo-Ottoman army, led by Sir Ralph Abercromby, launched an attack on March 21st, 1801. Despite Abercromby suffering a mortal wound during the conflict, the Battle of Alexandria ultimately resulted in an Allied victory (Mark, 2023). The fall of Cairo followed in June, and the prolonged siege of Alexandria finally resulted in Menou's surrender on September 2nd, 1801 (Mark, 2023). This signified the end of French control in Egypt, and the Treaty of Paris, signed on June 25th, 1802, formally ended hostilities between France and the Ottoman Empire.

Aftermath

After General Menou surrendered in Alexandria on September 2nd, 1801, the French troops stationed in Egypt faced a major change in their circumstances. The bulk of Menou's army confronted the prospect of returning to France, an operation that was efficiently carried out by the Royal Navy (Egyptian Campaign, n.d.). This repatriation effectively marked the conclusion of France's military presence in Egypt.

Napoleon's campaign in Egypt created an unexpectedly significant setback for the French. As part of the negotiated terms, the French were required to part with many of the cultural treasures that they had acquired during their campaign in Egypt. This included the Rosetta Stone — the content of which "was a decree in the name of king Ptolemy V Epiphanes" (Scalf, 2023), according to the Greek version of the text — and several other Egyptian antiquities that, to this day, hold profound historical and archaeological significance (Egyptian Campaign, n.d.). These valuable pieces were transferred into British possession as part of the conditions established after the French surrendered.

The French's decision to withdraw from Egypt was integral to the Peace of Amiens, an agreement that was finally reached on March 25h in 1802 (Egyptian Campaign, n.d.). This peace treaty served as the end of the Wars of the French Revolution, and temporarily ended the conflicts that had been going on in Europe for several years. The Treaty of Paris, which was signed on June 25th, 1802, officially ended the hostilities between France and the Ottoman Empire, and Egypt was, once again, under Ottoman rule (Egyptian Campaign, n.d.).

Although the French expedition in Egypt pretty much extinguished Napoleon's goal of establishing a Middle Eastern empire, it didn't end the conflicts taking place between the major European powers. The very next year hostilities between France and Britain resumed (Egyptian Campaign, n.d.). Naturally, this led to even more military confrontations and political maneuvers.

Chapter Summary

- 1797 — Napoleon was tasked with leading one-hundred-and-twenty-thousand men to invade Britain.
- April 1798 — Napoleon was entrusted with taking command of the newly formed Army of the Orient.
- June 12th, 1798 — The French military captured Malta.
- July 1st, 1798 — The French troops arrived in Egypt, and the very next day, they seized control of the coastal city of Alexandria.
- July 21, 1798 — Napoleon secured another victory at the Battle of the Pyramids.
- August 1-3, 1798 — Rear-Admiral Horatio Nelson secured a victory at the Battle of the Nile. This was mainly because the British reigned supreme when it came to naval forces at the time.
- October 20th, 1798 — News had reached Cairo that the Ottomans were putting together an army in Syria and were ready for an assault on Napoleon's forces.
- November 11th, 1798 — the insurrection had been successfully voided, which allowed Napoleon to redirect his attention toward the escalating threat in Syria.
- February 1799 — Napoleon led thirteen-thousand men out of Egypt.
- March 18, 1799 — Napoleon faces defeat at the Siege of Acre.
- August 23rd, 1799 — Napoleon set sail with only a handful of officers and scholars. He left the rest of his men stranded in Alexandria.
- September 2nd, 1801 — General Menou surrendered in Alexandria.
- March 25th, 1802 — The Peace of Amiens agreement was finally reached.

Segue

To put it simply, Napoleon Bonaparte's expedition to Egypt started with a bang and then fizzled out — partly due to poor planning, a lack of resources and reinforcements, and overconfidence on Napoleon's part. Surprisingly, he abandoned so many of his soldiers in Egypt, but his actions, perhaps, show that desperate times call for desperate measures. It didn't help that his soldiers were infected with the bubonic plague, either. The late 1700s were brutal in more ways than one!

In many ways, Napoleon was ruthless (consider him beheading the rebels in Egypt and piling their heads in the center of town). He made it abundantly clear that he wouldn't be trifled with (i.e. you didn't want to get on his bad side). His failure in Egypt wasn't due to a lack of effort. He probably expected too much of his soldiers (who are only human), and this ultimately led to his downfall. In the next chapter, I'll be delving into Napoleon's second campaign of Italy, and how he rose to power in 1799.

CHAPTER 4

Napoleon Bonaparte's Rise to Power

For centuries, Italy was comprised of several separate states. This was true even when the United States became independent from Great Britain in 1776 (*Unification of Italian States - Countries - Office of the Historian*, n.d.). In 1792, a war took place between Austria and the French, which we discussed in detail earlier. The French then invaded Italy, combined several Italian states, and made them into republics (*Unification of Italian States - Countries - Office of the Historian*, n.d.). In 1799, however, the French got kicked out by the Austrian and Russian armies, and the new republics fell apart.

When Napoleon rose to power, the French took over Italy again. Napoleon divided Italy into three parts: the northern areas (which joined the French Empire), the new Kingdom of Italy that was created under Napoleon's rule, and the Kingdom of Naples — first led by Napoleon's brother, Joseph Bonaparte, and later by his brother-in-law, Joachim Murat (*Unification of Italian States - Countries - Office of the Historian*, n.d.).

This was a significant moment in history for the French. Napoleon's second Italian campaign brought new ideas about government and society, which eventually led to the end of the old ways of doing things and feudalism (*Unification of Italian States - Countries - Office of the Historian*, n.d.). The ideas of freedom and equality became quite influential. The concept of nationalism had started to spread, too, effectively planting the seeds for Italian nationalism in the northern and central parts of Italy *(Unification of Italian States - Countries - Office of the Historian*, n.d.). In this chapter, we'll be discussing Napoleon's second Italian campaign in-depth. If you've been wondering why he was sent there in the first place or what he was trying to accomplish, you're in luck — I'll be covering everything you've ever wanted to know about this fascinating part of Napoleon Bonaparte's life below!

The Second Coalition

Napoleon's expedition to Egypt set the stage for a Second Coalition, which aligned Great Britain, Russia, and Turkey against France *(French Revolutionary Wars | Causes, Combatants, & Battles*, 1998). The Directory's foreign policy further fueled tensions, leading to a new alliance that included Austria. This compelled the French to defend their European conquests. In 1798, the Directory initiated additional conquests that Vienna viewed as violating the Campo Formio settlement. Blamed for a local uprising in Rome, the French Army marched on the city, proclaiming the Roman Republic in February 1798 *(French Revolutionary Wars | Causes, Combatants, & Battles*, 1998).

Responding to Napoleon's influence, the Directory occupied Switzerland, where the democratic party hoped for French pressure to force compliance from the ruling classes. The Directory ordered an advance on Bern in February 1798, which eventually resulted in its capitulation *(French Revolutionary Wars | Causes, Combatants, & Battles*, 1998). Simultaneously, France intervened in the internal affairs of satellite republics. They imposed constitutional changes in Holland and formed alliances, such as with the Cisalpine Republic.

At the Rastatt Congress, France sought territorial concessions beyond those that were agreed upon at Campo Formio. Napoleon was able to secure approval from the estates of the empire in March 1798 *(French Revolutionary Wars | Causes, Combatants, & Battles*, 1998). In September of 1798, with Turkish consent, a Russian fleet entered the

Mediterranean to liberate Malta and challenge French dominance. Rear-Admiral Horatio Nelson's victory at Aboukir Bay and Russian-Turkish alliances further complicated matters. Encouraged by British support, the Neapolitans attacked the Roman Republic and occupied Rome in November 1798 (*French Revolutionary Wars | Causes, Combatants, & Battles*, 1998). The Directory declared war on Naples, sending French troops to invade Sardinian Piedmont.

This was when Russia signed alliances with Naples and Britain, meaning that they committed to send troops in exchange for financial support (*French Revolutionary Wars | Causes, Combatants, & Battles*, 1998). Russia also allied with Turkey during this time. In early 1799, Russian forces attacked the Ionian Islands and captured Corfu in March. Despite earlier defensive alliances, Austria declared war on France in March of 1799 (*French Revolutionary Wars | Causes, Combatants, & Battles*, 1998).

Napoleon's Second Campaign in Italy

At the onset of the renewed general war, the Directory found itself inadequately prepared both in terms of numbers and resources. With the allies bringing in about twice as many troops, a French strategy would have concentrated forces in southern Germany and the Italo-Austrian frontier — anticipating the reinforcements from the conscription introduced in September of 1798 (*French Revolutionary Wars | Causes, Combatants, & Battles*, 1998b). However, the French chose to disperse their armies, and this led to defeats due to being outnumbered. The Austrians also failed to utilize their forces effectively.

The campaign's outset saw nearly eighty-thousand Austrians under the Archduke Charles in Bavaria, twenty-six-thousand in Vorarlberg, and forty-six-thousand in Tirol. Additionally, eighty-five-thousand troops were in Italy, with an expected sixty-thousand Russians joining soon. Facing this formidable coalition, the French had two-hundred-

and-ten-thousand men, with only one-hundred-and-thirty-six-thousand available against the Austrians (*French Revolutionary Wars | Causes, Combatants, & Battles*, 1998b). In Italy, the Directory struggled to allocate sufficient forces for defense. Despite the risks in the north, they retained troops under Jacques Macdonald in the south. Their goal was to conquer the Kingdom of Naples (*French Revolutionary Wars | Causes, Combatants, & Battles*, 1998b). The remaining forces were spread across Holland, the upper Rhine, and Switzerland.

Wanting to strike first before Russian reinforcements arrived, the French initiated offensives on all fronts. Jourdan moved between the upper Danube and Lake Constance, Masséna advanced toward Vorarlberg, and Schérer launched an offensive along the Adige (*French Revolutionary Wars | Causes, Combatants, & Battles*, 1998b). While Masséna secured some advantages, capturing Feldkirch proved critical for communication with the Army of the Danube. Jourdan, facing superior numbers, suffered a defeat at Stockach. By April 6th, Jourdan's retreat forced Masséna, now in command of both armies, to defend central Switzerland (*French Revolutionary Wars | Causes, Combatants, & Battles*, 1998b). In Italy, Schérer's initial success was short-lived, culminating in a retreat after defeat at Magnano.

In the north, Masséna's forces retreated to the Rhine, and the Austrians — led by Bellegarde and Hotze — pushed back Masséna's right wing through the Grisons. The Austrians left Masséna undisturbed, awaiting Russian reinforcements. In mid-August, the French right wing, led by Lecourbe, recaptured the St. Gotthard Pass, breaking the lull (*French Revolutionary Wars | Causes, Combatants, & Battles*, 1998b). The Austrians then sent Charles and a portion of his army to less significant operations on the middle Rhine, leaving Hotze and Korsakov to contain Masséna.

In Italy, Joubert replaced Moreau, and the French faced defeat at Novi on August 15. Suvorov, leading a contingent to Switzerland, shifted the allied command. Charles's forces moving to Germany weakened the allies in Switzerland, allowing the French, with seventy-seven-thousand troops, to go on the offensive against fifty-five-thousand allies (*French Revolutionary Wars | Causes, Combatants, & Battles*, 1998b). In the second battle of Zürich (September 25), Masséna was victorious, and this drove the Russians northward. Hotze was defeated by Soult southeast of Lake Zürich on the same day. Pursued by the French, the Russians retreated to Ilanz. Emperor Paul recalled the Russians on October 23rd (*French Revolutionary Wars | Causes, Combatants, & Battles*, 1998b).

Around the same time, an Anglo-Russian expedition to Holland, starting on June 22nd, 1799, aimed to free the Low Countries from French control. However, the only success was the surrender of Dutch ships (*French Revolutionary Wars | Causes, Combatants, & Battles*, 1998b). The French halted the allies' advance at Bergen, and after a defeat at Castricum, the Duke of York signed the convention of Alkmaar for the evacuation of his forces on October 18th (*French Revolutionary Wars | Causes, Combatants, & Battles*, 1998b).

The final blow to the coalition came in 1800, with Napoleon's victory at Marengo in Italy on June 14th and Moreau's triumph at Hohenlinden in Germany on December 3rd (*French Revolutionary Wars | Causes, Combatants, & Battles*, 1998b). The Directory was blamed for resuming these hostilities. This very likely set things up for Napoleon's military dictatorship, eventually culminating in his coup of 18–19 Brumaire year VIII (November 9–10, 1799), when he established himself as the first consul of France (*French Revolutionary Wars | Causes, Combatants, & Battles*, 1998b).

Napoleon Serves as the First Consul of France

By the time Napoleon Bonaparte hit the age of thirty, people knew him as "le petit tondu," thanks to his short and closely cropped hair (*Napoleon I | Biography, Achievements, & Facts*, 2023). Despite being on the smaller side (sources state that he was between 5'2" and 5'7" —

which was actually above average height for a French man back then) (McIlvenna, 2023), he had the confidence of a military champion, and (almost) always managed to come out on top. People were counting on him to bring back peace, calm things down in France, and solidify the political and social gains of the Revolution.

As we've learned, Napoleon was smart, made decisions on the fly (which usually — but not always — worked in his favor, and worked tirelessly. He imposed a dictatorship over France, but he disguised it with the constitution of the year VIII (December 25, 1799), written by clergyman Emmanuel Joseph Sieyès (*Napoleon I | Biography, Achievements, & Facts*, 2023). Unlike the ones before it, this constitution didn't talk about the "rights of man." Instead, it kept Revolution fanatics satisfied by stating that the sale of national property was a done deal and kept laws against émigrés in place (*Napoleon I | Biography, Achievements, & Facts*, 2023).

The first consul, which was mostly Napoleon himself, had a whole lot of power under this new constitution. Napoleon was given the responsibility of picking ministers, generals, and anyone important (*Napoleon I | Biography, Achievements, & Facts*, 2023). Even though the three legislative assemblies were supposed to be chosen by the vote of the people as a whole, the first consul was essentially destined to get his way no matter what. The constitution was approved by a vote in February 1800, which ensured that Napoleon stayed in charge (*Napoleon I | Biography, Achievements, & Facts*, 2023).

What Did Napoleon Do as First Consul?

Napoleon led the Consulate in making lasting changes to how France was run, and these changes ended up being more impactful than even the Constitution. At the core of the government was the Council of State, which the first consul started and often managed. This group didn't just make new laws; it also acted like a court for administrative matters (*Napoleon I | Biography, Achievements, & Facts*,

2023). Overseeing the administration of départements were the prefects — kind of like the intendants from back in the day. They made sure that laws were followed and helped to centralize power.

The judicial system went through a major shift — instead of electing judges, the government picked them. This ensured that they couldn't be removed from office. The police were reformed, and the financial side of things improved, too (*Napoleon I | Biography, Achievements, & Facts*, 2023). Special officials took over collecting direct taxes from municipalities, and the franc became stable. These officials even created the Banque de France, which was owned by both shareholders and the state (*Napoleon I | Biography, Achievements, & Facts*, 2023). Education went through a major transformation, too. Secondary education took on a semi-military structure, and university faculties were reinstated. Unfortunately, primary education didn't get as much attention (*Napoleon I | Biography, Achievements, & Facts*, 2023).

Even though Napoleon wasn't all that into religion, he agreed with Voltaire that people needed some kind of religious structure. Despite once considering becoming a Muslim in Egypt, he saw the importance of religious peace in France (*Napoleon I | Biography, Achievements, & Facts*, 2023). As early as 1796, while negotiating with Pope Pius VI in Italy, Napoleon tried to get the pope to take back his statements against French priests who supported the Civil Constitution of the Clergy, which made the church national (*Napoleon I | Biography, Achievements, & Facts*, 2023). Pope Pius VII, being more agreeable than the previous pope, signed the Concordat of 1801, making peace between the church and the Revolution. This agreement acknowledged the freedom of worship and the secular state (*Napoleon I | Biography, Achievements, & Facts*, 2023). The pope recognized the French Republic, asked former bishops to resign, and let the first consul pick new prelates who were then appointed by the pope. Rome even officially recognized the sale of clergy property.

Civil law started back in 1790 and finally got sorted under the Consulate with the Napoleonic Code. This legal framework solidified some of the big wins of the Revolution — like individual liberty, freedom of work and conscience, the secular state, and equality before the law (*Napoleon I | Biography, Achievements, & Facts*, 2023). It also protected property owners and gave more freedom to employers (while, unfortunately, not paying much attention to the rights of employees). Divorce stuck around, but women only got limited legal rights (*Napoleon I | Biography, Achievements, & Facts*, 2023).

The military went through serious changes during the Consulate, too. The first consul kept the recruitment system from the Revolution but made some alterations, like creating the Academy of Saint-Cyr for infantry officers, for example. This made it easier for kids from regular families to join the military (*Napoleon I | Biography, Achievements, & Facts*, 2023). The École Polytechnique, which started with the National Convention, was turned into a military school for artillery and engineers. Despite all the changes in education, Napoleon still believed in the speed and agility of his soldiers. He chose not to pay much mind to the new technical advancements in the military that were coming out at the time (*Napoleon I | Biography, Achievements, & Facts*, 2023).

Why Did Napoleon Put His Hand in His Coat?

The hand-in-waistcoat gesture has deep historical roots. It originates from the idea of gentlemanly restraint and is often linked to notions of nobility (Lowndes, 2020). Its symbolic significance dates back to ancient Greece, where the orator, Aeschines, advocated for restricting hand movement being the proper way to speak in public (Lowndes, 2020).

You've likely seen portraits of Napoleon Bonaparte with his hand in his coat. This gesture serves as a tool of propaganda (Lowndes, 2020). Jacques-Louis David's famous 1812 painting of Napoleon in his study is a notable example. In these depictions, Napoleon is portrayed as a humble and diligent leader, countering the negative image of him as a tyrant — especially prevalent outside of France, where he was often perceived as ill-tempered (Lowndes, 2020). The hand-in-waistcoat pose became a recurring theme in depictions of Napoleon during his lifetime and continued to be associated with him long after his death.

The lasting appeal of this gesture can be attributed to its adoption as a portraiture cliché during the early days of photography. Its dignified connotations, combined with the practicality of maintaining a steady pose during the long exposure times of early photography, made the hand-in-waistcoat stance a popular choice (Lowndes, 2020). As a result, it not only symbolized nobility and restraint but also transcended different artistic mediums. It's no wonder that this pose has become so iconic.

Napoleon Bonaparte's Battle Tactics and Influences

As the First Consul of France, Napoleon wanted to reclaim northern Italy, which had fallen back under Austrian control due to several defeats by Austrian and Russian forces in 1799, and the subsequent Austrian invasion of Lombardy and Liguria in April of 1800 (National Gallery of Victoria, n.d.).

During his second Italian Campaign, Napoleon came up with a creative strategy. Leading the Reserve Army, which was made up of about fifty-thousand soldiers, he orchestrated a bold march over the Swiss Alps into Northern Italy, eventually emerging unexpectedly behind Austrian lines (National Gallery of Victoria, n.d.). In a carefully planned move, Napoleon personally guided the French forces through the Swiss Alps. We can draw comparisons to the legendary feats of historical figures like Charlemagne and Hannibal (National Gallery of Victoria, n.d.).

Hannibal, who was celebrated for his military successes in ancient times, famously led the Carthaginian Army — including thirty-seven war elephants — through Alpine passes in 218 BCE (National Gallery of Victoria, n.d.). Even more meaningful to Napoleon, however, was Charlemagne's Alps-crossing invasion of northern Italy in 773 CE (National Gallery of Victoria, n.d.). By personally leading his soldiers, Napoleon not only replicated these historical events but also helped to improve morale among his troops. Despite favorable weather conditions during the crossing, Napoleon, in a letter to other consuls, discussed the challenges that he and his troops faced against "ice, snow, difficulties, and avalanches" (National Gallery of Victoria, n.d.).

Completing the Alpine crossing and circumventing the Austrian fort at Bard in just fifteen days, Napoleon emerged on the Lombardy plains on May 30th, 1800 (National Gallery of Victoria, n.d.). Prepared to face the Austrian Army, he confronted them in the Battle of Marengo on June 14th, 1800. Initially confronted with the possibility of Austrian victory, the timely arrival of General Desaix — one of Napoleon's best officers — with reinforcements turned the tide, despite Desaix falling in battle (National Gallery of Victoria, n.d.). Following this, Napoleon initiated peace negotiations on his terms, once again securing a narrow victory.

Charleville or Brown Bess?

Napoleon's soldiers did not use rifles and instead chose to use the Charleville 1777 revolutionnaire musket. Why, you might ask? Well, that's an excellent question, and I'll be discussing the answer below. For context, the British, at the time, were using the Brown Bess British Musket. The Brown Bess musket — particularly the Short Land Pattern and Long Land Pattern Muskets — was considered to be an impressive .75 caliber firearm, and it was featured in a lot of different models (Kiley, 2020).

During the American Revolutionary War, the Short Land Pattern became the standard, eventually replacing the phased-out Long Land Pattern. French muskets, distinguished by their year of manufacture rather than origin, gained the moniker 'Charleville' in the United States (Kiley, 2020). Many of these muskets were supplied to the Continental Army. With a .69 caliber, the French musket was characterized by eighteen French balls (equal to one pound). The Royal Army's last model was the 1777 musket, which was refined in the System of the Year Nine (1800-1801) and further improved in the Year Thirteen (1804-1805) (Kiley, 2020).

Both the Brown Bess and the 'Charleville' muskets were excellent in their ways. In the War of the Revolution, the Continental Army initially employed the Brown Bess, but upon receiving French musket shipments, they favored the 'Charleville,' despite its smaller ball size (Kiley, 2020). As a result, the 'Charleville' became the standard-issue musket for the Continental Army. The 1795 model Springfield musket, an outstanding firearm, drew inspiration (and may have, quite frankly, been directly copied) from the French model 1777 musket. This model served as the standard-issue musket during the War of 1812 (Kiley, 2020). It's also worth mentioning that the exploration of small arms from that period included a lot of different firearms, like fusils, carbines, mousquetons, dragoon muskets, pistols, rifled long arms, and rifled pistols (Kiley, 2020).

What Did the People and Governments Think of Napoleon and Empress Josephine?

In 1795, when radical Parisians opposed the new Convention constitution and threatened to attack government offices in the Tuileries, Barras called on Napoleon to stop the uprising. Napoleon's success in suppressing the insurgency brought him into the limelight within the Directory. During this period, Barras might have influenced Napoleon's interest in Rose (also known as Josephine). This eventually led to their marriage in March of 1796 (National Gallery of Victoria, n.d.).

The Bonaparte family expressed quite a bit of hostility towards Josephine. The Corsican ideal of a woman clashed with Josephine's characteristics, as she was perceived as immodest, wasteful with money, and easy-going but emotional (National Gallery of Victoria, n.d.). Despite being thirty-two with two children from her first marriage, the Bonapartes tried to distance themselves from her. Needless to say, this made things… awkward, for lack of a better word.

Josephine, described as dark-haired, and dark-eyed, with a clear complexion and a delicate figure, wasn't conventionally beautiful but was admired for her grace and charm (National Gallery of Victoria, n.d.). Despite Napoleon's initial infatuation and passionate letters to her, Josephine was pretty reserved in her affections. After their wedding, Napoleon left to lead the French Army in Italy, and Josephine found solace in her lover, Hippolyte Charles (National Gallery of Victoria, n.d.). Napoleon, shocked by her infidelity, considered ending the marriage. However, Josephine's emotional appeals and her children's pleas persuaded him to reconsider.

As Napoleon sought power and control in Egypt, Josephine acquired the estate of Malmaison. She eventually turned it into a magnificent property with a botanical garden, featuring specimens from around the world (National Gallery of Victoria, n.d.). Malmaison remained Josephine's residence until her death. With Napoleon's increasing influence, he was able to place his family members in critical positions across the Empire. Josephine's daughter, Hortense, married Napoleon's brother Louis — who became the King of Holland (National Gallery of Victoria, n.d.). Josephine's son, Eugène, served as Bonaparte's loyal deputy and held titles like "French Prince," "Prince of Venice," and "Viceroy of Italy" (National Gallery of Victoria, n.d.).

Chapter Summary

- 1798 — The Directory initiated additional conquests that Vienna viewed as violating the Campo Formio settlement.
- February 1798 — The Directory ordered an advance on Bern, which eventually resulted in the city getting captured.
- September 1798 — With Turkish consent, a Russian fleet entered the Mediterranean to liberate Malta and challenge French dominance.
- November 1798 — Encouraged by British support, the Neapolitans attacked the Roman Republic and eventually occupied Rome.
- 1799 — Russian forces attacked the Ionian Islands, and captured Corfu's in March. Despite earlier defensive alliances, Austria declared war on France in March of 1799.
- April 6th, 1799 — Jourdan's retreat forced Masséna, now in command of both armies, to defend central Switzerland. In Italy, Schérer's initial success was short-lived. This culminated in a retreat after defeat at Magnano.
- October 18th, 1799 — The French halted the allies' advance at Bergen, and after a defeat at Castricum, the Duke of York signed the convention of Alkmaar for the evacuation of his forces.
- October 23rd, 1799 — Emperor Paul recalled the Russians.
- June 14th, 1800 — Napoleon achieved victory at Marengo in Italy.

Segue

Napoleon Bonaparte rose to power rather quickly — and at a young age, too — which was quite unusual. At this point, he was getting the hang of leading a large army and was a master of military strategy. Upon becoming Emperor of France (which I'll be discussing, in-depth, in the next chapter), he crowned his wife, Josephine Empress, despite her infidelity. We'll be talking more about Napoleon's time as Emperor next, so don't go anywhere!

CHAPTER 5

The Crowning of an Emperor

In Notre Dame Cathedral in Paris, France, Napoleon Bonaparte assumed the title of Napoleon I, officially becoming the first French emperor in a thousand years. Pope Pius VII bestowed upon Napoleon the crown — a symbol of authority that the thirty-five-year-old conqueror of Europe placed upon his head ("Napoleon Crowned Emperor," 2010).

As we've learned, Napoleon had risen through the ranks of the French Revolutionary Army in the late 1790s, establishing himself as one of history's finest military strategists. The year 1799 witnessed France intertwined in conflicts with much of Europe. As I discussed previously, after returning from his Egyptian campaign, Napoleon took on an important role in the French government, steering the nation away from its imminent collapse ("Napoleon Crowned Emperor," 2010). His ascent to the position of first consul was the beginning of a detailed reorganization of the French military.

In 1802, Napoleon introduced the Napoleonic Code — a revolutionary legal framework that reshaped French law. Building on this, he proclaimed the establishment of the French Empire in 1804 ("Napoleon Crowned Emperor," 2010). Napoleon's visionary leadership propelled France's territorial influence by 1807, stretching from the River Elbe in the north to the Italian peninsula in the south, and from the Pyrenees to the Dalmatian coast ("Napoleon Crowned Emperor," 2010). This extraordinary expansion solidified Napoleon's legacy as not only a talented military figure but also a statesman. In this chapter, we'll be delving into Napoleon's time as the Emperor of France — a position that was honestly well-earned. Unfortunately, not everything went according to plan for Napoleon during this time, and he was eventually exiled to the Island of Elba. I'll be talking about this, too, so stick around!

The Painting in the Louvre

Painted by Jacques-Louis David between 1805 and 1807, *The Coronation of Napoleon* is a colossal neoclassical masterpiece measuring 9.79m x 6.21m (Da Costa, 2022). Functioning as a historical narrative and a propaganda tool, this artwork portrays the coronation ceremony of Emperor Napoleon Bonaparte and serves as a dramatic representation of the opulence associated with the new imperial regime at the time (Da Costa, 2022).

In 1804, at the age of thirty-five, Napoleon, who was enjoying immense popularity in France, was declared Emperor (Da Costa, 2022). Naturally, he wanted to have a grand religious ceremony to wrap up the festivities. Napoleon's actual coronation occurred on December 2, 1804, at Notre Dame Cathedral in Paris, prompting Napoleon to commission Jacques-Louis David, the emperor's main painter, to immortalize the event on canvas (Da Costa, 2022).

David spent two years painting this monumental piece in the church of Cluny. He utilized over two-hundred figures to create a virtual gallery of portraits. He was keen on accuracy. David even took notes for those he couldn't draw during the ceremony, which turned the process into a lively event where people were clamoring to be painted and included in the historic artwork (Da Costa, 2022).

Central to the painting is Napoleon and his wife Josephine, positioned at the apex of a pyramid formed by a large golden cross. The composition symbolically represents a convergence of two worlds: the sacred realm, led by the Pope on the right, descending to meet the secular world on the left, with Napoleon serving as the bridge between the divine and the earthly (Da Costa, 2022). The cross is meant to serve as a visual representation and reminder of this convergence.

As I mentioned before, this painting serves a dual purpose: reportage and propaganda. Although David wanted to capture the reality of the event in his painting, he had to take liberties to satisfy Napoleon's preferences (Da Costa, 2022). For example, Napoleon's mother, who disapproved of the ceremony, is portrayed as a central figure, smiling and elegantly dressed, even though she did not attend. The Pope, who reluctantly attended, is depicted blessing the crown with an uplifted arm, a gesture that was added at Napoleon's insistence (Da Costa, 2022).

Despite the grandeur depicted in the painting, historical accuracy was stretched quite a bit. The coronation took place in the ravaged Notre Dame Cathedral, which was damaged during the French Revolution (Da Costa, 2022). David, however, painted the cathedral's interior as sumptuous and majestic, completely glossing over the recent history of destruction — again, at Napoleon's insistence.

So, *The Coronation of Napoleon* is not just a neoclassical painting; it's an official piece of propaganda that was specifically designed to immortalize the memory of Napoleon's coronation ceremony. Napoleon himself, upon seeing the completed work, expressed immense satisfaction, declaring it a "relief" with remarkable truth (Da Costa, 2022). You can see this painting yourself in the Louvre Museum in Paris, France. If you ever get the opportunity to take a trip there, it's worth stopping by the museum and taking a gander at this masterpiece!

Napoleon Bonaparte is Crowned Emperor

The coronation of Napoleon Bonaparte as Emperor of the French took place on December 2nd, 1804, within the sacred confines of Notre-Dame de Paris cathedral as we just learned above. This solemn event was quite significant, as it served as a legitimizing ceremony for

Napoleon's rule. It also served as the inception of the First French Empire, which spanned from 1804 to 1814 and had a brief resurgence in 1815 (Mark, 2023). It also solidified the establishment of the imperial Bonaparte Dynasty.

The ceremony was meant to be both sacred and secular; the presence of Pope Pius VII, who served from 1800 to 1823, played a major role and coupled with the Concordat of 1801, symbolized the reconciliation between France and the Catholic Church (Mark, 2023). Simultaneously, the coronation acknowledged a secular dimension. It emphasized the notion that Napoleon's authority was rooted in the consent of the people.

Napoleon's coronation ceremony was unique. He incorporated elements from different historical periods — drawing from the rites of the Carolingian Dynasty, the traditions of the Ancien Régime, as well as certain aspects of the First French Republic (Mark, 2023). This amalgamation of rituals not only added to the grandeur of his coronation ceremony but also helped to establish Napoleon as a legitimate ruler.

You may be wondering what exactly led up to Napoleon being crowned the Emperor of France in 1804. Being crowned Emperor, after all, isn't something that "just happens" one day. Let's take a closer look at the events that led up to Napoleon's coronation below. We'll be delving a bit further into his time as First Consul here, as that ended up playing a major role in his rise to power.

THE FALL OF THE FRENCH KINGDOM

In the two centuries leading up to the French Revolution (1789-1799), absolute monarchy took hold in the Kingdom of France (Mark, 2023). Initially, French kings had authority within their local domains, mainly due to powerful local lords' competing interests. However, by the 17th century, power became centralized (exemplified by Louis XIV's tight grip). Louis XIV declared, "L'état, c'est moi!" ("I am the state!") (Mark, 2023), and that was that. After defeating the Fronde rebellion and eliminating any obstacles to his authority, Louis XIV's wars and reforms helped France become a prominent European power (Mark, 2023). His opulent palace at Versailles became the epicenter of court life — it created an almost mythical aura around the monarchy.

This governance model faced challenges during the reign of Louis XV (1715-1774), however, namely increased national debt and perpetual wars. Enlightenment ideas exposed social inequality behind the Ancien Régime's splendor, which contributed to simmering tensions that eventually erupted during the French Revolution of 1789 (Mark, 2023). Events like the Storming of the Bastille and the Women's March on Versailles played a part in dismantling the thousand-year-old French monarchy, too (Mark, 2023). The monarchy officially ended on August 10, 1792, with Parisians storming the Tuileries Palace.

The aftermath of this event didn't exactly bring smooth sailing. It brought the opposite. European monarchies formed an anti-French coalition, which sparked the French Revolutionary Wars (1792-1802) (Mark, 2023). French defeats led to the rise of the Jacobin-led Committee of Public Safety, dominated by Maximilien Robespierre, who ushered in the Reign of Terror. Robespierre's pursuit of a virtuous republic ended with his execution in 1794 (Mark, 2023). The French Directory then assumed power but faced public dissatisfaction due to instability, poverty, and attempted coups. The wearied population, craving stability, paved the way for Napoleon Bonaparte, who seized power in the Coup of 18 Brumaire in 1799 (Mark, 2023).

As First Consul, Napoleon claimed to embody the Revolution's ideals but gradually veered towards authoritarianism. Many viewed him as a legitimate leader, though, since he defeated the Austrians at the Battle of Marengo, effectively ending the Revolutionary Wars (Mark, 2023). Despite proclaiming meritocracy, he reintroduced elements of the Ancien Régime, reconciling with the Catholic Church and eventually reinstating a social hierarchy. In 1802, a plebiscite confirmed him as First Consul for life, making his position as a dictator official (Mark, 2023).

Napoleon Establishes a Hereditary Monarchy

Despite having the power of a king, Napoleon officially held the title of First Consul in a republic known for its regicidal tendencies. Recognizing the importance of securing his position in France and earning respect from other European monarchs, Napoleon knew that he needed to establish his hereditary monarchy. The opportunity presented itself in February of 1804 with the Cadoudal Affair, a royalist conspiracy led by Georges Cadoudal and backed by the British (Mark, 2023).

Their goal was to eliminate Napoleon and restore the exiled House of Bourbon to the French throne. In response, Napoleon positioned himself as the protector of revolutionary liberties, emphasizing that his demise could potentially lead France into chaos or back under Bourbon control (Mark, 2023). To keep this from happening, he advocated for a hereditary monarchy. This helped to ensure a smooth transition of power.

In late March of 1804, the Conseil d'État met to decide what the best title would be for Napoleon. Rejecting the "king" title (probably to avoid ties to the old Bourbon monarchy), and finding "prince" and "consul" too modest, they finally settled on "emperor," which was considered to be "the only [title] worthy of him and of France" (Mark, 2023). On May 18th, 1804, the Senate officially bestowed the imperial title upon Napoleon, who adopted the regnal name Napoleon I. Just eleven years after the trial and execution of Louis XVI, France shifted back to a hereditary monarchy — just as Napoleon hoped it would. Napoleon's popularity and promises to protect French liberties gained widespread support. Once again, this was evident in a plebiscite that overwhelmingly approved the imperial transition, though its credibility was rather questionable with a 99.93% approval rating (Mark, 2023).

By 1804, most former republican leaders who could have opposed Napoleon's coronation were either deceased or discredited. Those with enough influence to challenge him were tactically appeased with titles. Right after being declared emperor, Napoleon appointed honorary and active "marshals of the empire," including loyalists like Louis-Alexandre Berthier and Joachim Murat — as well as potential rivals, such as Jean-Baptiste Jourdan and Jean Bernadotte — who were placated to prevent any potential opposition (Mark, 2023). As summer approached, the political scene seemed stable enough for Napoleon to start planning his coronation.

Napoleon's Coronation Ceremony

On the morning of Sunday, December 2nd, 1804, guests gathered at the cathedral, seeking refuge under a neo-Gothic wooden awning to avoid the falling snow as they awaited the commencement of Napoleon's coronation ceremony (Mark, 2023). Around four-hundred-and-sixty musicians and choristers — including the imperial chapel, Feydeau Theatre, and the Opéra — made the cathedral come alive, no doubt setting the tone for this grand event. The doors opened, and guests, presenting invitations to ninety-two ticket collectors, were ushered to their seats by soldiers (Mark, 2023). Among the attendees were significant French figures and members of the diplomatic corps — excluding representatives from the United Kingdom (then at war with France), Russia, and Sweden (protesting the recent execution of the Duke of Enghien) (Mark, 2023). The Pope was carried in by twelve grooms in red damask. Talk about making an entrance!

At 10 a.m., artillery salvoes signaled Napoleon and Josephine's departure from the Tuileries Palace, drawing attention to their grand carriage drawn by eight white horses (Mark, 2023). The procession, which was led by Marshal Murat (the governor of Paris), included

Napoleon's family and advisors adorned with new titles. As the clock struck 11 a.m., the procession arrived at Notre Dame. Napoleon, in a crimson velvet mantle lined with ermine and adorned with golden bees, emerged from his carriage and, assisted by his brother Joseph, put on his coronation robe. Empress Joséphine wore a similar robe, which was carried by Napoleon's three sisters (Mark, 2023).

Entering the cathedral at 11:45 a.m., the emperor and empress were greeted by the Archbishop of Paris, who sprinkled them with holy water before they took their designated places (Mark, 2023). Despite the lengthy celebration making everyone feel a bit weary, Napoleon managed to maintain propriety. The climactic moment featured the unveiling of Napoleon's crown — a new creation that resembled that of Charlemagne — as he placed it on his head (Mark, 2023). Joséphine, kneeling before him, was also crowned. Once again, this scene has been immortalized in the painting by Jacques-Louis David.

Following the crowning, Pope Pius VII blessed the emperor and empress, after which Napoleon delivered his coronation oath. He pledged to maintain the integrity of the Republic's territory, uphold the laws of the Concordat, ensure freedom of worship, and political and civil liberty, as well as govern for the well-being and glory of the French people (Mark, 2023). Artillery salvoes and cheers of "Long live the emperor!" followed, concluding the ceremony. The imperial procession then paraded through the streets of Paris, accompanied by the papal procession, while soldiers lined the streets, holding back crowds of people who were eager to catch a glimpse of their new emperor (Mark, 2023).

Napoleon's "Grande Armee"

The Napoleonic army operated through three primary branches: artillery, infantry, and cavalry. The army also had an engineering corps and health service *(Napoleon's "Grande Armée" (1) - Napoleon.org*, n.d.).

We already know that Napoleon was quite talented when it came to artillery. He used cannon warfare tactics, while the infantry — made up of grenadiers, riflemen, cuirassiers, and skirmishers — fought on foot using muskets (*Napoleon's "Grande Armée" (1) - Napoleon.org*, n.d.). The mounted cavalry, which included dragoons, cuirassiers, carabiniers (these were soldiers armed with carabines or muskets — they usually rode on horseback), lancers, chasseurs, and hussars, wielded weapons like lances, sabres, swords, and pistols (*Napoleon's "Grande Armée" (1) - Napoleon.org*, n.d.). The engineering division focused mainly on constructing bridges for river crossings and fortifications for defense or sieges, while the health service, of course, consisted of surgeons and doctors who were dedicated to treating injured or ill soldiers.

Army recruitment relied mainly on conscription, with eligible young men between the ages of twenty and twenty-five years old being subject to a lottery system (provided, of course, that they were in good health and didn't have any disabilities that would prevent them from being able to fight). Regiments included a mix of young recruits and seasoned veterans, and training emphasized marching, obedience, weapon use, and proper equipment maintenance (*Napoleon's "Grande Armée" (1) - Napoleon.org*, n.d.). Promotion was primarily based on experience, though acts of exceptional bravery would sometimes accelerate a soldier's advancement through the ranks, too.

The Garde impériale was an elite unit that was responsible for Napoleon's protection, both on the battlefield and during his travels. Enlisting in the Garde impériale required a soldier to be at least 5'8" tall, and they had to have a minimum of ten years of service in another army corps. They also had to have the ability to read and write, which is what set the Garde impériale apart from other Napoleonic army units Garde impériale. In the 19th century, Napoleon responded to England's opposition to France's expansionist policies by organizing a massive military camp at Boulogne in 1803 (*Napoleon's "Grande Armée"*

(1) - Napoleon.org, n.d.). This signaled that he was preparing for a potential invasion of England.

The strategically located port of Boulogne accommodated between one-hundred-and-fifty-thousand and two-hundred-thousand soldiers and formed the core of the Grande Armée (*Napoleon's "Grande Armée" (1) - Napoleon.org*, n.d.). The camp witnessed extensive engineering projects — including docks, barracks, and roads — alongside training in naval embarkment and disembarkment. Despite his plan for an English invasion, by August 1805, Napoleon shifted his focus to continental Europe (*Napoleon's "Grande Armée" (1) - Napoleon.org*, n.d.). This was mainly due to Austria's alliance with Russia and their preparations for war. The Boulogne camp effectively provided Napoleon with a well-prepared and highly-trained army for any upcoming conflicts, though.

What Did Napoleon Do For France as Emperor?

Napoleon's goal wasn't to roll back time to the days of Louis XVI; instead, he retained several changes brought about by the French Revolution (*The French Revolution and Napoleon*, n.d.). He prioritized laws that would strengthen the central government while also staying in line with the goals of the revolution. His main focus was on economic stability — which eventually led to the creation of an efficient tax collection system and a national banking structure (*The French Revolution and Napoleon*, n.d.). These measures not only helped to ensure a more consistent tax supply but also facilitated much better economic control. Napoleon also dismissed corrupt officials and established lycées (government-run public schools) to train officials based on merit (*The French Revolution and Napoleon*, n.d.).

While he preserved several revolutionary changes, Napoleon did things a bit differently when it came to religion. He signed a concordat with Pope Pius VII to restore the Church's position without giving it control over national affairs (*The French Revolution and Napoleon*, n.d.).

This concordat gained a lot of support from the organized Church and the majority of the French population as well. Napoleon considered the Napoleonic Code — a system of laws that standardized legal principles and corrected injustices — to be his most significant achievement. The Napoleonic Code did limit individual rights, though. For example, it restricted the freedom of speech and press that was established during the Revolution and reintroduced slavery in French Caribbean colonies (*The French Revolution and Napoleon*, n.d.).

Napoleon, being an extremely ambitious man, didn't just want to rule France. He wanted to gain control over Europe and reassert French power in the Americas (*The French Revolution and Napoleon*, n.d.). Planning to build a western empire, his vision included Louisiana, Florida, French Guiana, and the French West Indies. Central to this plan was the sugar-producing colony of Saint Domingue (now Haiti) on Hispaniola (*The French Revolution and Napoleon*, n.d.). Despite initially responding to revolutionary ideas in Saint Domingue, Napoleon's attempt to restore the colony failed due to disease and particularly resilient rebels. So, he decided to sell the entire Louisiana Territory to the United States in 1803 (*The French Revolution and Napoleon*, n.d.). This helped him secure funds for European operations as well as a means to challenge Britain.

Shifting his focus to Europe, Napoleon annexed territories, established puppet governments, and faced opposition from Britain, Russia, Austria, and Sweden (*The French Revolution and Napoleon*, n.d.). With strategic brilliance, he achieved several victories and facilitated peace treaties with Austria, Prussia, and Russia (*The French Revolution and Napoleon*, n.d.). However, Napoleon went through a major naval defeat in 1805 during the Battle of Trafalgar. This resulted in British naval supremacy (once again), which caused Napoleon to abandon his plans to invade Britain. By 1812, Napoleon controlled most of Europe, but things were more unstable than they seemed at the time.

Ultimately, Napoleon would contribute significantly to the collapse of the French Empire in 1814.

Emperor Bonaparte's Greatest Enemies

By now we know that Napoleon was a significant figure in early 19th-century Europe. He left a lasting impact on the Napoleonic period, which is identifiable by the wars from 1803 to 1815 bearing his name. Despite Napoleon's prominence and popularity in France, he had a lot of enemies. One of his main adversaries, whom I mentioned in a previous chapter, was Admiral Horatio Nelson, whose Royal Navy indirectly influenced Napoleon's downfall (Szekler, 2023). Nelson's victories, especially at the Battles of the Nile and Trafalgar, demonstrated just how much of a naval threat the British were at the time. The Battle of the Nile in 1798 significantly weakened Napoleon's forces in Egypt, which, as we know, eventually led to him abandoning his soldiers in Alexandria. The British victory at Trafalgar in 1805 also thwarted Napoleon's plans to invade England (Szekler, 2023).

Another one of Napoleon's opponents was the Duke of Wellington, who was dubbed "the sepoy (a Persian-derived term from the word "sipahi," or a professional Indian infantryman) general" by Napoleon (Szekler, 2023). Napoleon thought this to be an insult, and frequently sneered at Wellington. Chances are, though, he was quite intimidated by Wellington's military prowess. Wellington showed his defensive skills during the Peninsular War, which eventually culminated in the Battle of Waterloo in 1815. He used the Waterloo battlefield to his advantage (don't worry — I'll be talking about the Battle of Waterloo in more detail later) which — along with the Prussian intervention — played a major role in the French defeat (Szekler, 2023).

Though less famous than Wellington, Archduke Charles of Austria was quite a competent general, too. In 1809, he outmaneuvered Napoleon at the Battle of Aspern-Essling (Szekler, 2023). Despite this victory, a fallout with Emperor Francis I ended up eroding Charles's trust and influence. Tsar Alexander of Russia — a notable ruler in continental Europe — had a rather complicated relationship with Napoleon. Having been defeated at Austerlitz in 1805, Alexander later allied with Napoleon (Szekler, 2023). He ended up turning against him in 1812, though, which Napoleon wasn't too happy about. His use of scorched earth tactics, along with the harsh Russian winter and disease, led to Napoleon's invasion of Russia failing in June of 1812 (Szekler, 2023).

It's also worth talking a little bit about Austrian diplomat Klemens von Metternich, who had temporarily made peace with Napoleon after seeing how much damage Austria had suffered during the Napoleonic Wars. Really, though Metternich was waiting for an opportunity to regain Austrian influence (Szekler, 2023). The disastrous French invasion of Russia provided that opportunity, and Metternich's diplomatic skills helped Austria achieve its goals during the peace conference at Vienna in 1815 (Szekler, 2023).

Napoleon's adversaries — whether on land or at sea, in battles or diplomacy — contributed to the various challenges that Napoleon faced during his reign as Emperor of France. Most of his adversaries played roles in his eventual downfall. Perhaps, having so many enemies weighed on him, and the pressure was too much for him to handle over time (not that Napoleon would have ever admitted this).

WHICH COUNTRIES OPPOSED NAPOLEON'S RULE?

The countries neighboring France, at the time, considered Napoleon to be a big problem — and it's not difficult to see why. Napoleon ruled for fifteen years, wrapping up the influence of the French Revolution in the late 1700s and early 1800s. His main goals were to establish a strong dynasty in France and create a European empire dominated by the French (*History of Europe | Summary, Wars, Map, Ideas, & Colonialism*, 2023). He consistently made smart moves —

declaring himself emperor, creating a new aristocracy, and staying in almost constant conflict with Britain, Prussia, and Austria (*History of Europe | Summary, Wars, Map, Ideas, & Colonialism*, 2023).

Until 1812, his military campaigns were mostly successful, despite a few strategy slip-ups. Napoleon's France took over lands, applied revolutionary laws, and set up satellite kingdoms across Europe. This illustrated just how far-reaching his rule was. However, after 1810, Napoleon ran into trouble. His empire faced hostility, especially in Spain, where a guerrilla movement started, and in Russia, which turned from an ally to an adversary during the disastrous 1812 invasion (*History of Europe | Summary, Wars, Map, Ideas, & Colonialism*, 2023). Things went downhill from there and ultimately led to a coalition forming in 1813. In 1814, France fell to invading forces, and Napoleon was sent into exile (which I'll be talking more about in a later chapter). Despite having a dramatic comeback in 1815, the Battle of Waterloo finally signified the end of his reign.

In France, Napoleon acted like a dictator and introduced new laws that improved equality at the time (*History of Europe | Summary, Wars, Map, Ideas, & Colonialism*, 2023). Internationally, his conquests spread French revolutionary laws, breaking down the power of the church and aristocracy in places like Belgium, western Germany, and northern Italy. Furthermore, the changes made to the European map due to Napoleon's influence were not only major, but lasting (*History of Europe | Summary, Wars, Map, Ideas, & Colonialism*, 2023).

When Napoleon consolidated territories in Germany and Italy (effectively getting rid of divided states), it fueled nationalism in both Spain and Poland. Even Prussia and Russia, less influenced by new ideas, made political changes to strengthen themselves against Napoleon (*History of Europe | Summary, Wars, Map, Ideas, & Colonialism*, 2023). The Congress of Vienna in 1814–15 aimed to bring stability back to Europe, confirming that regional states were simply buffers against French expansion and redistributing territories. The Treaty of

Vienna, though a letdown for nationalists pushing for a new Germany and Italy, wasn't harsh on France (*History of Europe | Summary, Wars, Map, Ideas, & Colonialism*, 2023). The main goal of the treaty was to balance power, and this created a relatively peaceful time for over half a century.

Chapter Summary

- August 10th, 1792 — The French monarchy officially ended with Parisians storming the Tuileries Palace.
- European monarchies formed an anti-French coalition, which sparked the French Revolutionary Wars (1792-1802).
- 1799 — Napoleon Bonaparte seized power in the Coup of eighteen Brumaire.
- 1802 — A plebiscite confirmed Napoleon as First Consul for life, making his position as a dictator official.
- December 2nd, 1804 — The coronation of Napoleon Bonaparte as Emperor of the French took place within the sacred confines of Notre Dame de Paris Cathedral. He was thirty-five years old. His wife, Josephine, was crowned as Empress. During this time, Napoleon also formed his "Grande Armee."
- 1805-1807 — Jacques-Louis David painted *The Coronation of Napoleon*, which is now hanging in the Louvre in Paris.
- 1805 — Napoleon's plans to invade England were thwarted due to the British victory at Trafalgar.
- 1809 — Archduke Charles of Austria outmaneuvered Napoleon at the Battle of Aspern-Essling.
- 1812 — Napoleon invaded Russia. The results of this invasion were disastrous for the French.

Segue

There's one thing you can't deny about Napoleon Bonaparte: he worked hard to get what he wanted in life. It's no wonder that he crowned himself Emperor of France in 1804. He felt like he deserved that crown, and in many ways, he truly did deserve it. While serving as the emperor, he did quite a lot for France. Not only did he improve economic stability, but he prioritized laws that would ultimately strengthen the central government while also aligning with the goals of the revolution.

As usual, things were going quite well for him — until 1812, when he decided to invade Russia. I'll be discussing his long road to Moscow very soon, but first, I'd like to talk a bit more about the role that his wife, Josephine, played as Empress of France between 1804 and 1812. I'll also be talking about why they separated as well as why Napoleon eventually remarried. By taking a look at his personal life, we can get an even better sense of who he was as a person, so let's dive right in!

CHAPTER 6

A New Empress

Empress Josephine — originally known as Marie-Joseph Rose de Tascher de la Pagerie — was born on June 23, 1763, at the Tros-Îlets plantation in Martinique (*Empress Josephine (1763-1814) - Napoleon.org*, n.d.). As a child, she went by Rose and was the eldest daughter of a well-off French family. At the age of ten, she was sent to the Dames-de-la-providence convent in Fort-de-France for an education that was supposed to make her a suitable match for a rich family's son (*Empress Josephine (1763-1814) - Napoleon.org*, n.d.). This led her to tie the knot with Alexandre de Beauharnais when she was sixteen years old. The ceremony took place on December 13th, 1779, in Noisy-le-Grand, just outside of Paris.

Her first marriage hit a rough patch, which isn't surprising considering she was so young at the time. This resulted in her separating from Alexandre de Beauharnais in 1785 without getting an official divorce (*Empress Josephine (1763-1814) - Napoleon.org*, n.d.). Rose, now facing financial struggles, had to sell her jewelry to make ends meet. Things got so rough that she and her daughter had to go back to Martinique for two years.

The French Revolution of 1789 brought both hope and danger to Rose's life. Returning to Paris in 1790 with her daughter, she reunited with her husband amid revolutionary chaos. Alexandre, who had a successful political career, became president of the constituent assembly in 1791. However, the turbulent political climate during the

Reign of Terror led to his arrest in 1794 for alleged political plotting (*Empress Josephine (1763-1814) - Napoleon.org*, n.d.). Although Alexandre faced execution, Rose narrowly avoided the guillotine due to the downfall of Maximilien Robespierre (a French lawyer and statesman) in July of 1794 (*Empress Josephine (1763-1814) - Napoleon.org*, n.d.).

Having been freed in August, Rose remained in Paris, navigating the unpredictable political landscape of the time. She built connections with especially influential figures, like Paul Barras — a future leader of the Directory (*Empress Josephine (1763-1814) - Napoleon.org*, n.d.). In 1795, she crossed paths with the one and only Napoleon Bonaparte. Despite their age difference and her status as a mother of two, they shared a common ambition (which I'll be discussing in more detail below).

They were married on March 9th, 1796 — the same year that Napoleon was appointed as commander-in-chief of the army of Italy. The woman who was once Rose from Martinique had become Empress Josephine, and she played more of a role in Napoleon's rise to power than most people realize. As I mentioned before, we'll be delving into the marriage of Napoleon and Josephine in this chapter. We'll also be talking a bit more about what was brewing in Europe during this time.

Why Did Napoleon Marry Josephine?

Napoleon, who had become a general at a young age, found it challenging to command officers who were much older than himself. Unhappy with this situation, he became determined to marry an older, wealthy woman — enter Josephine. After his success at the Battle of Toulon and protecting the Directory from the Paris mob; Paul Barras (a prominent figure in France at the time), noticed Napoleon's military genius. Seizing the opportunity, Barras orchestrated a scheme to marry off his mistress, Marie-Josephe-Rose de Beauharnais (once again, this is Josephine), to the young general (Schneider, 2005).

At a party thrown by Barras, Josephine (as she later became known to Napoleon) actually — unwittingly — played a role in Barras' plan. She enchanted Napoleon. He was captivated by her beauty, aristocratic background, and apparent wealth, and after the party ended, Barras encouraged Napoleon to pursue Josephine as a potential wife (Schneider, 2005). This would give Napoleon the financial security he needed, so he began his pursuit, "renaming" her Josephine since he disliked her original name (Schneider, 2005). Although Josephine initially played along, she remained resistant to marrying Napoleon. Faced with the challenge of supporting two mistresses, Barras pressured Josephine by threatening to cut her off financially. Fearing financial hardship and worried about her children, Josephine reluctantly agreed to marry Napoleon (Schneider, 2005).

The couple married shortly before Napoleon left for Italy. At this point, Napoleon genuinely loved Josephine. Josephine, however, hated Napoleon (partly because he "renamed" her, perhaps?), and found him dreadfully boring (Schneider, 2005). In Napoleon's absence, Josephine ended up having several affairs, meanwhile feigning affection in response to his letters. At the time, Napoleon wanted her to join him in Italy, but Josephine couldn't stand the idea of being around him. She even fabricated a pregnancy, hoping that it would make him stop requesting her presence (Schneider, 2005).

Napoleon's officers, upon returning to Paris, heard rumors about Josephine's infidelity. Murat, who was sent by Napoleon to bring Josephine to Italy, became ensnared in her web of lies (Schneider, 2005). Fearing Napoleon's return to France, Barras instructed Josephine to join her husband, which put an end to her affairs. When she arrived in Italy, Josephine claimed that she'd had a miscarriage, leaving Napoleon devastated over the loss of their supposed child (Schneider, 2005). So, it seems that while Napoleon initially married Josephine because of her looks, wealth, and age, he ended up falling in love with her. Despite eventually being forced to join Napoleon in Italy, it didn't take long for Josephine to return to her old ways.

Why Did Napoleon Separate From Josephine?

Ultimately, Josephine was unable to produce an heir for Napoleon, and this led to their separation in 1810 (National Gallery of Victoria, n.d.). After splitting from Josephine, Napoleon married Marie-Louise of Austria. This wasn't just about having a child to carry on his legacy, but also making friends with Austria for France's sake (National Gallery of Victoria, n.d.). Napoleon didn't forget about Josephine, though. He made sure she was taken care of, providing her with some money as well as the house at Malmaison (National Gallery of Victoria, n.d.).

Surprisingly, they stayed in close contact. This was, perhaps, evidence of the fact that there was a real emotional connection between them. While Josephine (mostly) despised Napoleon, she still may have felt for him. If you've ever been in a complicated (albeit tumultuous) relationship, you can probably relate! When Louis XVIII took charge in Paris, Josephine was able to get back into the mix, playing host to important people and cozying up to the new rulers. Sadly, she wasn't doing great health-wise by then. On May 29th, 1814, Josephine died from pneumonia at the age of fifty-one (National Gallery of Victoria, n.d.). It is widely believed that her last words mentioned "Bonaparte," "Elba," and "the King of Rome" (National Gallery of Victoria, n.d.).

Napoleon's New Marriage

Let's talk about Marie-Louise of Austria, and the reasons why Napoleon married her. We already know that he desperately wanted an heir, but why did he marry Marie-Louise out of all people? Marie-Louise de Habsburg-Lorraine, born in Vienna on December 12th, 1791, came from an important family. Her parents, Francis II and

Maria Theresa of Naples, were connected to Marie-Antoinette (*MARIE-LOUISE OF AUSTRIA - Napoleon.org*, n.d.). Despite her family being exiled in 1805, Marie-Louise had a fairly regular, happy upbringing with different caretakers. She disliked France, though, and had a deep hatred for Napoleon, whom she called the "Corsican ogre" (*MARIE-LOUISE OF AUSTRIA - Napoleon.org*, n.d.) This makes sense because Napoleon had caused a lot of destruction in Austria, as mentioned in previous chapters.

BUILD-UP TO THE IMPERIAL MARRIAGE

In 1809, when Marie-Louise was eighteen, she heard rumors that Napoleon, fresh off beating Austria again, was looking for a new wife. At first, the idea of being the Empress of France didn't sit well with her. She thought Napoleon wouldn't ask because he was scared of being turned down and because her dad, Francis II, wouldn't push for something so important (*MARIE-LOUISE OF AUSTRIA - Napoleon.org*, n.d.). Once again, she also didn't *like* Napoleon all that much. Despite worrying, she said she'd sacrifice her happiness for the good of the State. Her dad had his minister, Metternich, tell her about the arranged marriage, and even though it wasn't what she wanted, Marie-Louise accepted it without being bitter. Things moved fast after that, with the marriage contract being signed on March 8th, 1810, and the official wedding happening in Paris on April 2nd (*MARIE-LOUISE OF AUSTRIA - Napoleon.org*, n.d.).

THE BIRTH OF THE KING OF ROME

When she married Napoleon, Marie-Louise became Empress of France for the next four years. Their son, the "Roi de Rome," was born on March 20th, 1811 (*MARIE-LOUISE OF AUSTRIA - Napoleon.org*, n.d.). Finally, Napoleon had an heir! In 1813, when things got messy in Russia and Napoleon was away, Marie-Louise acted as regent in France. As the enemy got close to the capital, Napoleon came back briefly before leaving again on January 25th, 1814, never to see his wife and kid again (*MARIE-LOUISE OF AUSTRIA - Napoleon.org*, n.d.).

Meanwhile, Marie-Louise was sent to the Loire Valley with her son, Napoléon François Joseph Charles Bonaparte. She tried convincing Napoleon to let her go with him to Elba, but instead, he sent her to Austria, hoping she could help him and his family (*MARIE-LOUISE OF AUSTRIA - Napoleon.org*, n.d.). Even though he promised they'd meet again, Marie-Louise's actions later on suggested that she was reconsidering their relationship, even at that point.

After Waterloo

After France lost at Waterloo in 1815, Marie-Louise, drawn in by the Comte de Neipperg, gave up on the idea of going back to Napoleon (*MARIE-LOUISE OF AUSTRIA - Napoleon.org*, n.d.). Even when he came back in triumph, she didn't show any interest in reuniting with him. The defeat at Waterloo convinced her that her future was somewhere far from France, and this ultimately led her to go in a different direction than her husband.

What Was Brewing in Europe During This Time?

We discussed this briefly already, but let's take a closer look at what was happening in Europe during this time, shall we? The weakening position of the French triggered a significant turn of events known as the Sixth Coalition from 1813 to 1814. Prussia and the United Kingdom teamed up with Russia, declaring war on France, while Austria initially stayed on the sidelines due to complex relationships within the Imperial families (McLean, n.d.). During this turmoil in 1813, Marie Louise took on the role of Regent as Napoleon engaged in military campaigns in Germany (as stated before). Of course, her regency was largely symbolic. The most important decisions were still being dictated by Napoleon and then carried out by his top officials (McLean, n.d.).

Despite Marie-Louise's attempts to sway her father, the Emperor of Austria, to align with France, Austria eventually joined the coalition against Napoleon (McLean, n.d.). Throughout this challenging period, Marie-Louise kept up a correspondence with Napoleon; updating him on the escalating calls for peace in Paris and the provinces. In January of 1814, Marie-Louise found herself reappointed as Regent (McLean, n.d.). This was when Napoleon had to bid farewell to her and their son before hurrying off to face the Allied invasion from the north.

As the Allies approached Paris, Marie-Louise hesitated to leave, holding onto the belief that — as the daughter of the sovereign of Austria and a member of the Allied nations — she would be treated with respect. Additionally, she saw her son as a potential heir to the French throne if Napoleon were to die in battle. She eventually (and reluctantly) departed, though, failing to foresee her father's actions to dethrone Napoleon and strip her son of his claim to the French crown (McLean, n.d.). In April of 1814, she was taken aback when the Senate, influenced by Talleyrand, announced Napoleon's deposition (McLean, n.d.).

Following Napoleon's abdication in April of 1814, the Treaty of Fontainebleau sent him into exile on the island of Elba. Marie-Louise, however, retained her imperial rank and style and was granted rule over the duchies of Parma, Piacenza, and Guastalla, with her son designated as the heir (McLean, n.d.). When Napoleon made a comeback in 1815, the Allies once again declared war. Marie-Louise, now requested by her stepmother to pray for the success of the Austrian armies, rejected the disrespectful invitation. Napoleon's final defeat at the Battle of Waterloo in 1815 led to his exile to Saint Helena, and he made no further attempts to personally reach out to Marie-Louise (McLean, n.d.). The Congress of Vienna recognized her as the ruler of Parma, Piacenza, and Guastalla but imposed restrictions on her ability to bring her son to Italy. Furthermore, she was designated Duchess of Parma for her lifetime only, as the Allies wanted to prevent any descendants of Napoleon from making hereditary claims over Parma (McLean, n.d.).

Chapter Summary

- December 13th, 1779 — Josephine (at the time known as Marie-Joseph Rose) married Alexandre de Beauharnais when she was just sixteen years old.
- 1789 — The French Revolution brought hope and danger to Josephine's life. She returned to Paris in 1790 with her daughter and reunited with her husband during revolutionary chaos.
- 1795 — Josephine crossed paths with Napoleon Bonaparte for the first time.
- March 9th, 1796 — Josephine married Napoleon the same year that he was appointed as commander-in-chief of the army of Italy.
- December 2nd, 1804 — Napoleon is crowned Emperor and Josephine is crowned Empress of France.
- 1810 — Josephine and Napoleon separate after they are unable to conceive a child together.
- May 29th, 1814 — Josephine died from pneumonia at the age of fifty-one.
- March 8th, 1810 — Marie-Louise of Austria and Napoleon got married so that Napoleon could have an heir and make friends with Austria (in theory, at least).
- 1813, when things got messy in Russia and Napoleon was away, Marie-Louise acted as regent in France.
- January 25th, 1814 — Napoleon came back briefly but never saw his wife and kid again thereafter.
- 1815 — France lost at Waterloo and Napoleon was exiled on the island of Saint Helena.

Segue

It seems that Napoleon had quite the love life — despite neither of his wives enjoying his company all that much (especially at first). Napoleon was a man who got what he wanted, and that included women. This was also, definitely, a sign of the times. Marie-Louise was essentially forced into a marriage with Napoleon, which wasn't uncommon in the late 1700s and early 1800s. More than anything, Napoleon wanted to have an heir who could carry on his legacy. His son, Napoleon II (also known as Napoléon François Joseph Charles Bonaparte), became the King of Rome, the Duke of Reichstadt, and then the Prince of Parma in Italy. In the next chapter, I'll be discussing Napoleon's long road to Moscow. This is probably the time in his life that he's most well-known for. It's quite an exciting story, so you'll want to stick around!

CHAPTER 7

Napoleon's Retreat From Moscow

In 1799, when Napoleon Bonaparte seized power, he achieved a series of military victories that firmly established his dominance over a significant part of Europe (as we're already well aware). His conquests extended to present-day Belgium and Holland, including substantial territories in Italy, Croatia, and Germany. Additionally, he established dependencies in Switzerland, Poland, and various German states (Greenspan, 2023). Even in the face of guerrilla warfare in Spain, Napoleon maintained control over the country, eventually coercing Austria, Prussia, and Russia into forming alliances.

In 1806, Napoleon came up with the Continental System — an embargo aimed at punishing Britain by economically isolating the island nation (Greenspan, 2023). However, by the end of 1810, Czar Alexander I of Russia stopped being compliant with this system. He didn't like the way it was affecting Russian trade and the ruble's value. Alexander also imposed hefty taxes on French luxury goods and rejected Napoleon's proposal for a marital alliance involving one of his sisters (Greenspan, 2023).

Things had already become quite tense between France and Russia by that point anyway since Napoleon created the Duchy of Warsaw in 1807 (which was made up of Prussian land) (Greenspan, 2023). This move raised Alexander's concerns about the potential emergence of hostile Polish nationalism. Seeing Russia as a natural ally with no territorial conflicts, Napoleon wanted to, for lack of a better term, "teach Alexander a lesson" (Greenspan, 2023). In 1812, he assembled a huge European army, ranging from four-hundred-and-fifty-thousand to six-hundred-and-fifty-thousand Grande Armée soldiers crossing the Niemen River to face approximately two-hundred-thousand Russian soldiers (Greenspan, 2023).

Napoleon's goal was to force Alexander to negotiate with him. However, the Russians strategically withdrew from the battle and allowed the Grande Armée to capture Vilna on June 27th (Greenspan, 2023). An electrical storm struck that night, which caused casualties among troops and horses. The Grande Armée soldiers were starving, and many deserted Napoleon in search of food and plunder (Greenspan, 2023). Despite these setbacks, Napoleon kept his confidence up, and shared with his military advisors that he was determined to quell the "barbarians of the North" (Greenspan, 2023). He wanted to push them back into their territory, as this would supposedly keep them from meddling in the affairs of "civilized Europe" for the next quarter-century. Things didn't go as planned for Napoleon, however. In this chapter, we'll be taking a closer look at Napoleon's invasion of Russia and why it was ultimately the beginning of the end for him.

Napoleon's Russian Campaign

Napoleon Bonaparte's ill-fated invasion of Russia in 1812, famously portrayed in Leo Tolstoy's *War and Peace*, serves as a powerful symbol of the downfall that often awaits those who wield too much power. This historical event shares similarities with what happened to Charles XII of Sweden and Adolf Hitler in the 20th century. Interestingly, there's a common theme here powerful leaders meeting their match within the borders of the Russian Empire (*Napoleonic Satires*, n.d.). Despite some misunderstandings (once again, there's a lot of false information about Napoleon Bonaparte out there), Napoleon's campaign was well-thought-out and well-supplied. Its origins lie in Tsar

Alexander I's decision to abandon the Continental System and start trading with Britain (one of France's most formidable enemies at the time) (*Napoleonic Satires*, n.d.).

The preparations for the invasion started in January of 1811 and were in direct response to the Tsar's perceived disloyalty. As I mentioned previously, Napoleon quickly built up his impressive Grande Armée — totaling around seven-hundred-thousand soldiers — and positioned them along the Poland-Russia border. Interestingly, Russia chose not to immediately retaliate and instead formed the Sixth Coalition through a secret agreement with Sweden in March of 1812 (which also included Britain and rebel Spain) (*Napoleonic Satires*, n.d.). By May of the same year, Napoleon took charge of the Grande Armée that he had assembled in Poland and, on June 24th and 25th, crossed the Niemen River (*Napoleonic Satires*, n.d.). This signaled the beginning of Napoleon's Russian campaign.

While Napoleon publicly justified his mission as a means to eliminate the ongoing threat posed by Russia, his true motive was to reprimand the Tsar for breaking the continental blockade (*Napoleonic Satires*, n.d.). Napoleon's plan probably would have worked, had the Russian army not disrupted his strategic intentions by refusing to engage in battle. The main battle took place at Borodino on September 7th, 1812, and resulted in territorial gains for Napoleon (even though he lost a lot of soldiers) (*Napoleonic Satires*, n.d.). Shortly thereafter, Napoleon's army entered Moscow, which was abandoned and devastated due to the Russian forces implementing a "scorched-earth policy." In other words, the Russians burned all of their crops and resources so that Napoleon wouldn't be able to benefit from invading Moscow (*Napoleonic Satires*, n.d.).

As the French occupied the city, the harsh Russian winter set in. Yes, that's right — the weather made a huge difference (i.e. the French weren't prepared for it), and along with Tsar Alexander's stubborn refusal to negotiate for peace, ended up causing one of Napoleon's greatest failures. Napoleon had no choice but to retreat from Moscow in less than a month after his forces had "captured" it. The Russian winter, which was especially unforgiving, took a severe toll on the Grande Armée, with only a fraction — around one-hundred-thousand soldiers — returning to France (*Napoleonic Satires*, n.d.). Napoleon's strategic miscalculation would cost him in more ways than one, which I'll be talking about shortly.

Napoleon's Retreat

Napoleon initially planned a retreat to the south, but things took an unexpected turn, and his troops were forced to retrace their steps after coming across a resupplied Russian army at Maloyaroslavets (Greenspan, 2023). The situation grew increasingly dire as they found that all available forage along the path had been exhausted. Upon reaching Smolensk, the army faced another setback when they realized that stragglers had consumed whatever food was left. To add to their woes, a significant number of horses were perishing, and the Grande Armée had to contend with constant attacks from both flanks and the rear guard (Greenspan, 2023).

As if these challenging circumstances weren't enough, an unusually early winter descended upon them, bringing high winds, sub-zero temperatures, and heavy snowfall. On the harshest nights, thousands of men and horses succumbed to exposure. Desperation set in, leading soldiers to resort to unconventional measures — such as splitting open dead animals for warmth (Greenspan, 2023). In some instances, dead bodies were stacked in windows to act as insulation against the harsh cold. Napoleon became overwhelmed — understandably so.

In late November, the Grande Armée narrowly avoided complete annihilation when it crossed the freezing Berezina River, albeit leaving behind thousands of wounded soldiers (Greenspan, 2023). Following this close call, it became an every-man-for-himself situation, which prompted Napoleon to entrust the command to Joachim Murat and rush back to Paris amid rumors of a coup attempt (which I'll be discussing in a bit more detail below). By December 5th, the remaining members of the Grande Armée's rear guard had finally made their way back across the Niemen River, with, quite frankly, not much help from Napoleon whatsoever (Greenspan, 2023).

"An Army Marches on Its Stomach!"

Napoleon Bonaparte is often credited with the saying, "An army marches on its stomach," but there's no concrete evidence that he uttered those words. Similar to Marie Antoinette's famous "Let them eat cake," these quotes, even if attributed to them, might be more legend than reality (Martyris, 2015). Regardless, if Napoleon did express such sentiments, they would have rung hollow, given the challenging conditions his soldiers frequently faced. Surprisingly, despite being a great military leader, Napoleon overlooked the critical aspect of making sure that his army was adequately fed (Martyris, 2015). Granted, keeping an army that large well-fed was probably no easy task.

While the official orders for the Grande Armée's rations appeared to be sufficient on paper — comprising of soup, boiled beef, a roasted joint, and vegetables (without dessert) — real-world challenges, like bad roads and inclement weather, often disrupted the timely delivery of supplies to the soldier's campsites (Martyris, 2015). In the Italian campaign, where Napoleon rose to fame by defeating a much larger Austrian army, his soldiers had to resort to foraging or plundering nearby villages due to logistical issues. This was an accepted practice in military operations during that time, but it still couldn't have been a very pleasant experience for anyone involved.

The dire conditions faced by Napoleon's troops during his campaigns in Russia and Egypt made things even more complicated. In Egypt, the expedition was launched with such speed that there wasn't even time to issue water canteens (Martyris, 2015). The 55,000-strong army had to endure a grueling three-day march through scorching sands from Alexandria to Cairo without adequate provisions, which resulted in there being quite a few casualties from heat and thirst (Martyris, 2015). In Russia, the Grande Armée experienced starvation and extreme cold. Desperate soldiers resorted to eating horseflesh seasoned with gunpowder, while buzzards feasted on the corpses strewn along roads and battlefields (Martyris, 2015).

Despite the hardships and hunger that his soldiers faced, Napoleon kept eating his daily meals. Usually, his meals consisted of "white bread, Chambertin, beef or mutton," along with his favorite rice with beans or lentils (Martyris, 2015). However, his valet at the time, Louis-Joseph-Narcisse Marchand, claimed that during the famine in Russia, Napoleon ate like an ordinary soldier in a show of solidarity with his suffering troops (Martyris, 2015). Napoleon was pretty indifferent about what he ate. He often skipped meals and favored simplicity, even using his fingers to eat instead of utensils. His culinary preferences — such as roast chicken — were, perhaps, a reflection of his practicality. He was even content with diluted wine (Martyris, 2015).

Napoleon's disregard for his army's dietary needs — in combination, of course, with the harsh conditions his soldiers had to face during the campaigns in both Egypt and Russia — led to his downfall. This just goes to show that an army's success hinges on more than just military strategy. It also relies on the availability of sustenance for the soldiers on the front lines. Although Napoleon's soldiers were largely successful in Italy and Egypt (at the beginning of the Egyptian campaign, at least), they were only human. Napoleon could be "practical," but he could also be quite brutal, as we've already learned. He came to understand that an army needs plenty of sustenance to be successful, especially during a long campaign. This is where his supposed quote "An army marches on its stomach" comes from. It seemed, however, that Napoleon came to this realization too late.

Napoleon's Vulnerability is Exposed

As Napoleon licked his wounds after his Russian campaign, the rest of the world (or Europe, at the very least) realized something: For once in his life, Napoleon Bonaparte was *vulnerable*. His former allies (who were reluctant to be allied with him in the first place), such as Prussia and the Confederation of the Rhine quickly distanced themselves from his cause (*Napoleonic Satires*, n.d.). In December of 1812, sensing trouble, Napoleon left Russia, leaving his army behind — a move that was quite reminiscent of his earlier abandonment of his soldiers in Egypt. His return to Paris was triggered by a conspiracy led by the half-mad General Malet, who — fueled by rumors of Napoleon's demise in Russia — was threatening to overthrow him (*Napoleonic Satires*, n.d.). Even Napoleon's most hesitant allies were beginning to question their loyalty to him at this point.

Things only got worse for Napoleon from there. Prussia severed ties with him and joined forces with Russia. Northern Germany rebelled against Napoleonic rule, and under the leadership of Marshal Bernadotte, Sweden reinforced the coalition against Napoleon. Austria, while breaking its alliance with France, remained neutral until August, strategically positioning itself against Napoleon (*Napoleonic Satires*, n.d.). Not only that but the French were forced to evacuate Madrid. Suddenly, almost all of the major European powers were turning against him.

The alliance solidified in August of 1813 when Austria abandoned its neutrality to join efforts to expel Napoleon's forces from Germany (*Napoleonic Satires*, n.d.). Despite Napoleon's skillful military tactics in the campaigns of Germany in 1813 and France in 1814, the sentiment among his marshals and French legislators shifted. Ultimately, they recognized the inevitable loss of Napoleon's cause (*Napoleonic Satires*, n.d.). The pivotal "Battle of the Nations" at Leipzig in October of 1813 led to the collapse of the Confederation of the Rhine and the

Kingdom of Westphalia, which finally compelled Napoleon to retreat from Germany (*Napoleonic Satires*, n.d.).

Napoleon found himself fighting on two fronts, contending with Wellington's advance through northern Spain to the Pyrenees. As the Allies crossed the Rhine in January of 1814, and Murat, the king of Naples, defected in a desperate attempt to salvage his throne, Napoleon staunchly rejected all offers of peace (*Napoleonic Satires*, n.d.). Even a series of brilliant actions in eastern France in February of the same year couldn't prevent the relentless Allied advances from the east and south.

Wellington entered Bordeaux in March, Marshals Marmont and Mortier surrendered Paris to the Allies by the end of the month, and, after a last-ditch effort to preserve the dynasty by abdicating in favor of his son, Napoleon unconditionally abdicated on April 11th of 1814, through the Treaty of Fontainebleau (*Napoleonic Satires*, n.d.). Napoleon's family was placed under the custody of Francis I of Austria, and Louis XVIII ascended the throne as France was restored to its 1792 frontiers. Starting his exile on the island of Elba on May 4th, Napoleon had no choice but to face the reality of his diminished power and the irreversible course of events that had unfolded. The tables had turned, to say the least!

Chapter Summary

- 1806 — Napoleon came up with the Continental System.
- 1807 — Napoleon created the Duchy of Warsaw.
- 1810 — Czar Alexander I of Russia stopped being compliant with the Continental System.
- January 1811 — Napoleon started preparing to invade Russia.
- 1812 — Napoleon assembled a huge European army, ranging from four-hundred-and-fifty-thousand to six-hundred-and-fifty-thousand Grande Armée soldiers. They crossed the

- Niemen River to face approximately two-hundred-thousand Russian soldiers.
- June 27th, 1812 — The Russians withdrew from battle and allowed the Grande Armée to capture Vilna. An electrical storm struck that night, which caused several casualties among troops and horses.
- December 1812 — Napoleon retreated from Moscow, abandoning several of his troops. He did so partly because he'd heard rumors about a coup taking place in France.
- August 1813 — The alliance between the European powers solidified when Austria abandoned its neutrality to join efforts to expel Napoleon's forces from Germany.
- April 11th, 1814 — Napoleon abdicated through the Treaty of Fontainebleau. He was placed under the custody of Francis I of Austria and was exiled to the island of Elba a month later.

Segue

I've been hinting, throughout this book, that Napoleon's downfall may have been due to his overconfidence — at least in part. As you can see, there were a lot of reasons why things didn't pan out for Napoleon in Russia. His soldiers weren't prepared for the treacherous winter weather, and Napoleon could not provide them with enough food to survive, let alone thrive. Everything that *could* have gone wrong in Russia ended up going wrong. As I mentioned earlier, we've seen this happen with different world leaders in similar situations throughout history. Isn't it fascinating how history always repeats itself in one way or another? Perhaps, it's more terrifying than it is fascinating — but you know what I mean. In the next chapter, I'll be delving into the aftermath of what happened in Russia. Napoleon lost an entire empire and was forced to concede. How did he grapple with this? How did the political landscape change? We've got a lot to discuss when it comes to this part of Napoleon's life, so let's get into it.

CHAPTER 8

An Emperor Falls

The French invasion of Russia in June of 1812 was one of the most catastrophic military events in history. The tragedy becomes clear when we look at the numbers: out of almost seven-hundred-thousand French and allied troops who crossed the Niemen River, less than one-hundred-thousand made it back after six months (Mark, 2023). The survivors, just a small part of the original group, carried the physical and mental scars of their experience with them. Thousands dealt with the aftermath of frostbite and not having enough food, and a lot of them faced lasting disabilities. Almost half a million troops were affected, and at what cost?

Around one-hundred-thousand soldiers left during the retreat with Napoleon, while another one-hundred-and-twenty-thousand were captured. Russia became the final resting place for the remaining three-hundred-and-eighty-thousand, buried under the unforgiving Russian snow (Mark, 2023). It's difficult to say how many soldiers the Russians lost in total, but it's widely believed that around one-hundred-and-fifty-thousand Russian soldiers likely died from different causes, with at least twice that number getting hurt (Mark, 2023). The impact went beyond the military losses, however. An unknown number of Russian civilians faced the harsh consequences of the invasion, too. The total number of military and civilian deaths likely passed one million, which makes Napoleon's invasion of Russia one of the deadliest events in military history.

The aftermath of the Russian campaign affected all of Europe, and honestly left a lasting mark on history. Napoleon never fully recovered from this terrible event. While he quickly got more infantry conscripts, the losses in cavalry and artillery were too much to replace (Mark, 2023). At the same time, the Russian army, after successfully stopping the French invaders, didn't stop at the Niemen but kept going into Europe. With the help of the armies of Britain, Prussia, and Austria, they were able to start the War of the Sixth Coalition, which lasted from 1813-1814 (Mark, 2023). In this chapter, we'll be diving into the nitty-gritty details of the aftermath of Napoleon's failure in Russia and how this changed the political landscape of Europe at the time. Let's get started!

The War of the Sixth Coalition

A surviving unit of the Grande Armée was a Prussian corps obligated to fight for Napoleon under the terms of the Treaties of Tilsit in 1807 (Mark, 2023). General Johann von Yorck, its commander (and a Prussian patriot), sought to break free from French control. On December 31st, 1812, he signed an armistice with the pursuing Russian army. Although King Frederick William III of Prussia denounced Yorck's armistice, fearing French retaliation, several Prussian officers and ministers followed suit, renouncing their loyalties to Paris (Mark, 2023). On January 4th, 1813, the Russian army entered Königsberg, the capital of East Prussia, which prompted local authorities to declare war on Napoleon and initiate the formation of an army. Realizing that his country was headed for war, Frederick William reluctantly allied with the Russians on February 28th, 1813, through the Treaty of Kalisch, stipulating that Prussia and Russia would not negotiate with Napoleon independently (Mark, 2023).

The United Kingdom, which was seemingly locked in continuous conflict with France since 1803, welcomed the emergence of a potential Sixth Coalition and resumed its role as a financial supporter

(Mark, 2023). By promising to assist Sweden in acquiring Norway from Napoleon's ally, the Kingdom of Denmark-Norway, Britain successfully enlisted Sweden into the alliance. Austria, eager for Napoleon's downfall but wary of Russian dominance, remained neutral at first (as previously discussed). Austria offered an armed mediation, indicating its willingness to join the coalition if peace talks happened to fail. Simultaneously, Austria mobilized two-hundred-thousand troops from its Landwehr militia (Mark, 2023).

Napoleon returned to Paris on December 18th, 1812, a day after the public learned of the Grande Armée's demise. Despite the shock and the absence of most veteran soldiers occupied in Spain or lost in Russia, Napoleon quickly announced the formation of a new army of one-hundred-and-fifty-thousand men to confront the growing coalition against him. By April 1813, he managed to assemble this force, which was mostly made up of predominantly young and inexperienced conscripts. The army also lacked cavalry due to the loss of horses in Russia (Mark, 2023). Learning of the Russo-Prussian invasion of Saxony in April, Napoleon assumed command of his new Army of the Main on April 25th, leaving Empress Marie Louise as regent in Paris. He hoped that her ties to Emperor Francis I of Austria would discourage Austrian participation in the war, but Austria was determined to see Napoleon's downfall (Mark, 2023).

The Allies Ask Napoleon for an Armistice

On May 1st, 1813, Napoleon crossed the Saale River to come to the defense of Saxony. Tragically, on the same day, Marshal Jean-Baptiste Bessières, one of his most trusted commanders, was hit by a cannonball while scouting enemy positions (Mark, 2023). Needless to say, this dealt a considerable blow to the French morale. Going up against a ninety-thousand-man Russo-Prussian army at the Battle of Lützen on May 2nd, Napoleon was able to secure a slight victory, yet the absence of cavalry prevented him from fully capitalizing on his success as he wasn't able to pursue the retreating Allied forces (Mark, 2023). The Allies regrouped in Bautzen, and then faced Napoleon again on May 20-21, in the Battle of Bautzen. This battle resulted in another French triumph (Mark, 2023). Despite this, Napoleon couldn't annihilate the Allied army. The Allies retreated to Silesia, leaving a path open to Berlin. When French Marshal Nicolas Oudinot tried to seize the Prussian capital, he suffered defeat at the hands of Prussian General Friederich von Bülow during the Battle of Luckau on June 4th (Mark, 2023).

Tensions flared among the Allies as Prussia and Russia each blamed the other for setbacks at Lützen and Bautzen. Desperately needing time for reinforcement and resupply, the Allies approached Napoleon and asked him for an armistice (basically, a request to stop warring for a while). Surprisingly, Napoleon agreed, and the Pleischwitz Armistice was signed on June 4th (Mark, 2023). It only lasted until August 18th, so it's hard to say whether that was enough time to gather more soldiers and supplies. Napoleon, having lost forty-thousand men in the campaign, viewed the armistice as an opportunity to replenish his forces. However, in retrospect, the armistice robbed him of the chance to capitalize on his victories, mainly because it allowed the Allies to regroup and strengthen their military (Mark, 2023). Austria, honoring its promise of mediation, entered the fray on June 26th. Foreign minister Prince Klemens von Metternich met with Napoleon in Dresden (Mark, 2023). Metternich's peace terms demanded Napoleon's relinquishment of control over Germany, Poland, and Italy, and the restoration of Prussia to its pre-1806 status. When Metternich held firm, Napoleon, infuriated, declared, "So, you want war? I have already annihilated the Prussian army at Lützen; I have defeated the Russians at Bautzen; now you want your turn. Very well, we shall meet at Vienna" (Mark, 2023).

Upon rejecting Metternich's Dresden proposals, Napoleon faced Austria's entry into the Sixth Coalition on June 27th (Mark, 2023). He was nothing if not stubborn, that's for sure! Coalition leaders convened at Trachenberg to come up with a strategy, eventually settling on deploying half a million men across three major armies: the two-hundred-and-thirty-thousand-man Army of Bohemia commanded by Austrian Field Marshal Karl Philipp, Fürst von Schwarzenberg; the one-hundred-and-forty-thousand -man Army of North Germany led by Swedish Crown Prince Charles John; and the one-hundred-and-five-thousand -man Army of Silesia under Prussian General Gebhard Leberecht von Blücher (Mark, 2023). The Trachenberg Plan emphasized avoiding direct engagement with Napoleon, and instead focused on pressuring French flanks and communications. This plan also encouraged the destruction of forces led by Napoleon's marshals during separate missions (Mark, 2023). Charles John, drawing on his experience as a former French marshal, used his previous understanding of Napoleon's strengths and weaknesses to help the Allies come up with this strategic approach.

Invasion of France

As hostilities resumed on August 18th, 1813, the Allies set their Trachenberg Plan into motion. Marshal Oudinot, who was tasked with seizing Berlin, faced defeat by Charles John at the Battle of Grossbeeren on August 23rd (Mark, 2023). Simultaneously, on August 26th and 27th, Napoleon exploited an error by Schwarzenberg, engaging the Army of Bohemia in the Battle of Dresden. Although he was victorious here, his victory was quite lacking. The Allies, following the Trachenberg Plan, continued to challenge the French forces, and this eventually led to the defeat of Marshal Macdonald at the Battle of Katzbach on August 26th (Mark, 2023). When Marshal Ney attempted to capture Berlin, he fell into a trap set by Charles John, succumbing to defeat at the Battle of Dennewitz on September 6th (Mark, 2023).

The repeated defeats suffered by Napoleon's marshals proved costly — tens of thousands of troops lost their lives. Furthermore, the

Allies had disrupted French supply lines, exacerbating provision shortages for Napoleon's remaining soldiers (Mark, 2023). While pursuing the retreating Allies, Napoleon faced even more challenges. Commanders like Blücher and Charles John successfully avoided confrontation with him. What's more, Bavaria, his close German ally, defected to the coalition on October 8th. Frustrated, Napoleon withdrew to Leipzig, hoping to make a stand (Mark, 2023).

The Battle of Leipzig, also known as the "Battle of the Nations," took place from October 16th to 19th in 1813 (Mark, 2023). This battle was huge — it involved one-hundred-ninety-thousand French and three-hundred-and-eighty-thousand Allied troops. The Battle of Leipzig is said to be the largest battle in European history before World War I (Mark, 2023). Despite a stalemate on the first day, the odds eventually turned against Napoleon. Saxon and Württemberg troops switched sides, and the Allies received steady reinforcements. On October 19th, in a chaotic retreat, the French forces suffered significant casualties, with thousands stranded on the wrong side of the Elster River after a premature bridge explosion (Mark, 2023). The defeat at Leipzig, with sixty-thousand French casualties against around fifty-thousand for the Allies, destroyed any hope for Napoleon to win the war (Mark, 2023).

Napoleon's subsequent defeats on multiple fronts further weakened his position. By November 18th, 1813, the Allies declared the Confederation of the Rhine dissolved, and German states turned against Napoleon by providing troops to the coalition (Mark, 2023). Joachim Murat, seeking to retain his Kingdom of Naples, switched sides. Meanwhile, Napoleon's brother Joseph lost the Battle of Vitoria, leading to the fall of Bonapartist Spain (Mark, 2023). Wellington's invasion of Southern France continued, and by February 1814, Bordeaux surrendered to Wellington without resistance, raising the flag of the old Bourbon Dynasty (Mark, 2023).

In November of 1813, Metternich proposed peace terms through the Frankfurt Proposals. Offering Napoleon the retention of his throne and specific territories, the terms were deemed the best he could get. However, delayed and unresolved negotiations resulted in the withdrawal of the offer in December (Mark, 2023). Napoleon prepared to defend France, attempting to rally patriotic sentiment by permitting the banned republican anthem La Marseillaise and resurrecting the Jacobin refrain "La Patrie en Danger!" ("The fatherland is in danger!") (Mark, 2023) Despite his efforts, after two decades of war, French support for Napoleon waned. Most troops were conscripts, including many young recruits referred to as "marie-louises" (Mark, 2023).

The Allies invaded France in January 1814 and were met with determined resistance from Napoleon. His plan aimed to keep the Allied armies divided and wear them down with quick attacks. Victories, such as at the Battle of Brienne on January 29th and the Six Day Campaign against Blücher, once again demonstrated Napoleon's strategic genius when it came to war (Mark, 2023). However, Schwarzenberg's advance toward Paris prompted a shift in tactics. On March 20th, Napoleon faced a larger force at the Battle of Arcis-sur-Aube, which resulted in his defeat. The Allies intercepted crucial French military intelligence and arrived in Paris on March 30th, leading to the Battle of Paris on March 31st (Mark, 2023). The bloody conflict ended with parleys, and a provisional government, led by Talleyrand and Fouché, negotiated the restoration of the Bourbon Dynasty.

Meanwhile, Napoleon, at Fontainebleau, faced pressure from his marshals to abdicate for the good of France. On April 2nd, he sent Caulaincourt with an offer to abdicate in favor of his son, yet Marshal Marmont's surrender on April 4th forced an unconditional abdication on April 11th, 1814 (Mark, 2023). The Treaty of Fontainebleau granted Napoleon sovereignty over Elba and an annual income of two million francs. On April 20th, he bade farewell to his Imperial Guard before being exiled. This served as the end of the hostilities with the Treaty of Paris on May 30th, 1814 (Mark, 2023). France reverted to its 1792 borders, and the Congress of Vienna convened to redraw the map of post-Napoleonic Europe. However, the Napoleonic Wars were not concluded. On March 20th, 1815, Napoleon escaped from Elba and initiated the Hundred Days. Despite a brief return to power, he suffered defeat at the Battle of Waterloo on June 18th, 1815, which led to his exile on the island of St. Helena (Mark, 2023).

Chapter Summary

- January 4th, 1813 — The Russian army entered Königsberg, the capital of East Prussia, which prompted local authorities to declare war on Napoleon and initiate the formation of an army.
- February 28th, 1813 — Frederick William reluctantly allied with the Russians through the Treaty of Kalisch, stipulating that Prussia and Russia would not negotiate with Napoleon independently.
- April 1813 — Napoleon managed to assemble his force, which was mostly made up of predominantly young and inexperienced conscripts.
- May 1st, 1813 — Napoleon crossed the Saale River to come to the defense of Saxony.
- May 2nd, 1813 — Napoleon scored a slight victory over the Russo-Prussian army at the Battle of Lützen.
- June 4th, 1813 — The Pleischwitz Armistice was signed. The Allies and Napoleon attempted to regroup.
- August 18th, 1813 — As hostilities resumed, the Allies set their Trachenberg Plan into motion.
- August 26th, 1813 — The Allies defeated Marshal Macdonald at the Battle of Katzbach.

- October 16th-19th, 1813 — The Battle of Leipzig, also known as the "Battle of the Nations," took place. Napoleon was defeated.
- November 1813 — Metternich proposed peace terms through the Frankfurt Proposals.
- January 1814 — The Allies invaded France.

Segue

Napoleon's fall from power was swift and unforgiving. He remained determined and tried to keep his head above the water, despite everyone being against him. The Allies made all the right choices here, and Napoleon found himself floundering. He probably never should have invaded Russia in the first place, but as I mentioned before, he got a little *too* confident (which makes sense, because he had previously been quite successful). In the next chapter, I'll be discussing Napoleon's escape from exile and the one-hundred days that followed. We'll also be covering what happened at Waterloo, so you'll want to stick around!

CHAPTER 9

The 100 Days

The Hundred Days is an important period in French history, stretching from March 20th, 1815, when Napoleon came back to Paris after escaping his exile on Elba, to July 8th, 1815, when Louis XVIII returned to the French capital (The Editors of Encyclopaedia Britannica, 2023). The term "Hundred Days" was coined by the prefect of the Seine, comte de Chabrol de Volvic, as he welcomed the returning king in a speech (The Editors of Encyclopaedia Britannica, 2023).

Less than a year after his abdication on April 6th, 1814, and the onset of the Bourbon Restoration, Napoleon left his island exile in the Tyrrhenian Sea. He landed at Cannes on March 1st with a force of one-thousand-five-hundred men (The Editors of Encyclopaedia Britannica, 2023). Advancing towards Paris, he entered the capital just a week later, which prompted Louis XVIII to flee to Ghent on March 13th (The Editors of Encyclopaedia Britannica, 2023). In a bid to broaden his support, Napoleon introduced liberal changes to the Imperial Constitution. This persuaded some of his former adversaries, including Benjamin Constant, to rally behind him.

However, the international landscape was quite tense during this time. On March 25th, Austria, Britain, Prussia, and Russia allied against Napoleon. This laid the groundwork for a series of battles that eventually culminated in the decisive Battle of Waterloo on June 18th (The Editors of Encyclopaedia Britannica, 2023). Napoleon's failure at the Battle of Waterloo tends to be what he's most known for. It's a bit like a trainwreck that history lovers like myself can't look away from. In this chapter, we'll be talking about exactly what happened during the Hundred Days, and why Napoleon suffered such a significant loss at Waterloo.

How Did Napoleon Escape Exile?

During his exile in Elba, Austrian and French guards closely monitored Napoleon. Despite this surveillance, he was not entirely cut off; he received a multitude of letters from across Europe and stayed informed about global events through major newspapers. It was likely through these sources that he learned of Josephine's death on May 29th, 1814 (*Napoleon Bonaparte Study Guide: Exile and Escape | SparkNotes*, n.d.). On February 26th, 1815, Napoleon managed to elude his guards and escape from Elba. He skillfully avoided interception by a British ship and made a triumphant return to France.

Almost immediately, people and troops rallied around the reinstated Emperor (*Napoleon Bonaparte Study Guide: Exile and Escape | SparkNotes*, n.d.). French police forces were dispatched to apprehend him, but upon actually being in his presence, they knelt before him. Napoleon's return to Paris on March 20th, 1815, was met with jubilation. Again, this caused the new king, Louis XVIII, to flee to Belgium. Seizing the opportunity, Napoleon reclaimed the Tuileries (this is considered to be the beginning of "The Hundred Days") (*Napoleon Bonaparte Study Guide: Exile and Escape | SparkNotes*, n.d.).

Once again, in an attempt to bolster his support, Napoleon initiated minor reforms and pledged to establish a more liberal, democratic society. One of his most notable reforms during this period was the "Additional Act to the Constitution of the Empire," although the hollow nature of this reform (and others) did not go unnoticed, which ultimately led to a decline in Napoleon's backing (*Napoleon Bonaparte Study Guide: Exile and Escape | SparkNotes*, n.d.). Meanwhile, pro-Bourbon Royalists in Western France remained active. The news of Napoleon's escape from Elba sent shockwaves through the Congress of Vienna, where European powers were convening to determine the post-Napoleonic rearrangement of Europe. On March 13th, 1815, the nations represented at the Congress declared Napoleon an outlaw (*Napoleon Bonaparte Study Guide: Exile and Escape | SparkNotes*, n.d.).

Precursory Battles Leading Up to Waterloo

Napoleon, along with around one-thousand-five-hundred men, made a bold return to France, eventually landing at Golfe-Juan near Antibes on March 1st (*Timeline of the 100 Days - Age of Revolution*, 2015). Their rapid march towards Paris took them through towns like Cannes, Séranon, Castellane, Barrême, Malijai, Sisteron, Gap, and Corps. In a rather surprising turn of events, when soldiers of the 5th Regiment, who were initially ordered to intercept Napoleon, rallied to his cause as he approached them south of Grenoble, defiantly proclaiming, "Here I am. Kill your Emperor, if you wish!" (*Timeline of the 100 Days - Age of Revolution*, 2015). The soldiers then joined Napoleon on his march towards Paris.

On March 13th, 1815, Marshal Ney, who was originally tasked with arresting Napoleon, defected and joined him with six-thousand men — a fateful act of treason (*Timeline of the 100 Days - Age of Revolution*, 2015). Joachim Murat, King of Naples, and Napoleon's brother-in-law, declared war on Austria, aligning himself with Napoleon despite breaking a prior treaty between them. The Seventh Coalition, which, as stated previously, included Britain, Russia, Austria, and Prussia, pledged to mobilize substantial forces, each committing one-hundred-and-fifty-thousand men to defeat Napoleon (*Timeline of the 100 Days - Age of Revolution*, 2015).

On March 20th, 1815, Napoleon entered Paris. As we know, he was trying to build support for himself by introducing minor reforms and promising a more liberal, democratic society. However, the Allied forces remained steadfast in their opposition. Murat's defeat at the Battle of Occhiobello and the decisive Battle of Tolentino in May were considered to be major setbacks for the pro-Napoleon forces in Italy. Undeterred, Napoleon, leading a force of two-hundred-thousand, launched an offensive campaign on June 15th (*Timeline of the 100 Days - Age of Revolution*, 2015).

The Battle of Ligny on June 16th saw Napoleon defeating Prussian Field Marshal Blücher but falling short of destroying his forces. Simultaneously, Marshal Ney and Wellington fought in the inconclusive Battle of Quatre Bras (*Timeline of the 100 Days - Age of Revolution*, 2015). Amid these events, D'Erlon's 1 Corps wandered between battles, missing a critical opportunity to tip the scales in their favor. Blücher retreated towards Wavre, while Wellington strategically positioned his forces on the Mont St. Jean ridge south of Waterloo (*Timeline of the 100 Days - Age of Revolution*, 2015).

As the decisive Battle of Waterloo loomed on the horizon, Napoleon faced the challenge of confronting the converging British and Prussian armies. He knew that he was going to have to drive a wedge between them if he was going to obtain separate victories. The intricate maneuvering and clashes that happened next set the stage for a historic confrontation that unfolded on June 18th, 1815 — none other than the Battle of Waterloo (*Timeline of the 100 Days - Age of Revolution*, 2015). This was the climax of the Hundred Days and led to the ultimate downfall of Napoleon Bonaparte.

The Battle of Waterloo

During the Battle of Waterloo, Napoleon received intelligence that Wellington's army and the Prussians had withdrawn on divergent lines. Seizing the opportunity, Napoleon decided to advance on Wellington while dispatching Marshal Grouchy to pursue the retreating Prussians to his right (*Timeline of the 100 Days - Age of Revolution*, 2015). Adopting a blunderbuss strategy, Napoleon tried to employ artillery and frontal assaults to disable Wellington's center before the Prussians (around eighty-thousand in total) could join the fray from the northeast (*Timeline of the 100 Days - Age of Revolution*, 2015). Despite using this strategy, Napoleon delayed the attack until midday. He likely did so to let the ground dry for better artillery and cavalry maneuvering. This gave Blücher, the Prussian commander, ample time to rendezvous with Wellington later in the day, however (*Timeline of the 100 Days - Age of Revolution*, 2015).

The tactical command was unwisely delegated to the brave but impulsive Ney, who depleted his forces with unsupported cavalry charges on unbroken British squares. Ney failed to spike British guns, allowed excessive numbers to be drawn into Prince Jérôme's diversion at Hougoumont on the British right, and launched a premature final assault (*Timeline of the 100 Days - Age of Revolution*, 2015). Although Napoleon was somewhat responsible for refusing to reinforce Ney when the British center wavered, the day concluded around 8 PM with the resilient Allies (sixty-eight-thousand with one-hundred-and-forty-six cannons) halting the Imperial Guard's attempt to break through; delivering a sudden rifle volley into their flank (*Timeline of the 100 Days - Age of Revolution*, 2015). The French were defeated, and the non-arrival of Marshal Grouchy's forty-thousand French troops, coupled with Blücher's army advancing on Napoleon's right flank, further crushed French morale. Allied losses amounted to approximately twenty-two-thousand killed and wounded, with seven-thousands of those being Prussian, while French losses were around thirty-seven-thousand. The Prussians pursued the retreating French throughout the night (*Timeline of the 100 Days - Age of Revolution*, 2015).

Chapter Summary

- March 1815 — Napoleon came back to Paris after escaping his exile in Elba.
- March 13th, 1815 — Marshal Ney, who was originally tasked with arresting Napoleon, defected and joined him with six-thousand men. Napoleon was declared an outlaw by the nations represented at the Congress of Vienna.
- June 15th, 1815 — Napoleon, leading a force of two-hundred-thousand, launched an offensive campaign.
- June 16th, 1815 — The Battle of Ligny saw Napoleon defeating Prussian Field Marshal Blücher but falling short of destroying his forces.
- June 18th, 1815 — Napoleon lost at the Battle of Waterloo.

Segue

The Battle of Waterloo was tough for Napoleon for several reasons. He had quite literally just made his comeback, only to be crushed by the Allies once again. It's undeniable that he tried his hardest to secure power over France — and a lot of people *were* still willing to follow him. Still, though, there were far too many people who felt like Napoleon had to be taken down a few pegs (for lack of a better phrase). This was why he was ultimately exiled to Saint Helena, where he died on May 5th, 1821. I'll be going over his exile on Saint Helena as well as his death in the next chapter.

CHAPTER 10

A Second Exile

In the aftermath of his Waterloo setback, Napoleon confronted the harsh reality of abdication in Paris on June 22nd, 1815 (*From Waterloo to the Island of St Helena - napoleon.org*, n.d.). In a surprising twist, he abandoned his imperial ambitions in favor of his young son, who was just four years old at the time. However, the anticipated imperial legacy for his son, who had been hidden in Austria with Empress Marie-Louise since May 1814, never actually materialized. Instead, Louis XVIII, brother to the guillotined Louis XVI from the tumultuous days of the French Revolution, assumed the throne and ascended as the new King of France (*From Waterloo to the Island of St Helena - napoleon.org*, n.d.).

Relatively unfazed by the abrupt turn of events (at least on the surface), Napoleon left Paris on June 25th, 1815. He sought solace in Malmaison and shared a poignant farewell with his mother (*From Waterloo to the Island of St Helena - napoleon.org*, n.d.). Although he initially wanted to escape to the United States, Napoleon's plans were foiled by the French provisional government's failure to issue the promised passport (*From Waterloo to the Island of St Helena - napoleon.org*, n.d.). Consequently, he found himself on the secluded island of Aix, near Rochefort. His fate was in the hands of the British navy stationed there — which was very bad news for Napoleon.

Upon surrendering to the British forces on the Bellerophon, Napoleon expressed his willingness to submit to the protection of their prince and laws. As the British people eagerly gathered in small boats at the port of Torquay, Napoleon, now bearing the title of "General Bonaparte," became the object of both amusement and curiosity (*From Waterloo to the Island of St Helena - napoleon.org*, n.d.). News of his exile to St. Helena, a remote island under British rule in the Atlantic Ocean, reached Napoleon on July 31st, 1815, while he was at the port of Plymouth. Boarding the Northumberland on August 7th, he bid farewell to British shores on August 9th, never setting foot on the land that briefly harbored his adversaries (*From Waterloo to the Island of St Helena - napoleon.org*, n.d.). A grueling nine-week sea voyage concluded with his arrival on the desolate island of St. Helena on October 15th, 1815 (*From Waterloo to the Island of St Helena - napoleon.org*, n.d.). Here, he would spend the rest of his days, which is what we'll be talking about in this final chapter.

Life on the Island of St. Helena

When Napoleon got exiled to St. Helena, he wasn't alone — there were about twenty people with him. General Bertrand, who had previously been quite the big deal in the palace, joined him, along with General de Montholon with his family (*From Waterloo to the Island of St Helena - napoleon.org*, n.d.). Count Las Cases was with him too, as was General Gourgaud and plenty of workers, such as Louis Marchand, the butler, Cipriani, and Louis Etienne Saint-Denis, who was also known as "Ali Mamaluke" (*From Waterloo to the Island of St Helena - napoleon.org*, n.d.). Despite the British laying down the rules, Napoleon got to bring some of his belongings from his palaces back home (i.e. furniture, tableware, paintings, and even a portrait of his son). All things considered, it was a fairly cushy "exile."

When he first arrived, Napoleon stayed in a house called the Briars, which was owned by the Balcombe family. There he met Betsy, a lively fourteen-year-old from the family. Surprisingly, she wasn't afraid of Napoleon, and they hit it off. After a few months, they finished building another place called 'Longwood,' and on December 10th, 1815, Napoleon moved in (*From Waterloo to the Island of St Helena - napoleon.org*, n.d.). This was where Napoleon and his crew, including the Bertrand family who had their own house, stayed for the duration of Napoleon's life.

Napoleon had a routine on St. Helena. He ate good food, went horseback riding, and told his life story to his friends. Nights were for playing the piano, chess, cards, and digging into the massive collection of books that he'd brought along with him. He even tried his hand at gardening to shake things up (*From Waterloo to the Island of St Helena - napoleon.org*, n.d.). Exile, it seemed, was mostly pretty boring, which couldn't have been too easy for a man like Napoleon. Napoleon also wasn't allowed to roam freely. He had British eyes on him all the time, and his letters got checked before he was allowed to read them (*From Waterloo to the Island of St Helena - napoleon.org*, n.d.). Governor Sir Hudson Lowe was paranoid about Napoleon trying to escape again, so he had three-thousand guards patrolling the shores to make sure no one was able to sneak in (or out) (*From Waterloo to the Island of St Helena - napoleon.org*, n.d.).

Eventually, Napoleon kind of withdrew into Longwood, keeping visitors at a distance and spending more time by himself. He was anxious for news about his son during this time. Some of his friends left the island, like General Gourgaud in 1818 and Madame de Montholon in 1819 (*From Waterloo to the Island of St Helena - napoleon.org*, n.d.). Things got even lonelier for Napoleon, when, in December of 1816, Las Cases and his son got kicked off the island for trying to sneak out secret letters (*From Waterloo to the Island of St Helena - napoleon.org*, n.d.).

How Did Napoleon Bonaparte Die?

In the last six years of his life, Napoleon's health deteriorated, marked by frequent illness and a significant decline in his final six months. His doctor, Francesco Antommarchi, documented symptoms like severe abdominal pain, nausea, vomiting, night sweats, and progressive weakening, providing a detailed account of the emperor's physical decline. In 1821, Napoleon Bonaparte passed away in exile, leaving behind a lingering mystery surrounding his death. Despite his doctor citing stomach cancer as the cause on the death certificate, there are still a lot of doubts, among histories, regarding how he died (ABC News, 2007). Many have speculated about the possibility of foul play, suggesting poison as a potential culprit.

These suspicions gained traction with the discovery of locks of Napoleon's hair, which reportedly contained dangerous levels of arsenic. Researchers also delved into his valet's diaries, pointing out the surprisingly well-preserved state of Napoleon's body when exhumed in 1840 (ABC News, 2007). However, Dr. Robert Genta from the University of Texas in Dallas rejects the idea of this conspiracy, asserting that Napoleon genuinely succumbed to advanced gastric cancer (ABC News, 2007). Amid ongoing debates, Dr. Genta dismisses fanciful ideas about what might have happened had Napoleon escaped exile. Yes, it's true — the once powerful emperor was that sick. Even if he had returned to Paris, Dr. Genta argues that Napoleon's physical condition was so critical that his death would have been swift (ABC News, 2007). In other words, it was simply his time.

In 1840, Napoleon, who had been buried on Saint Helena Island since 1821, was moved to Les Invalides in Paris by the decision of King Louis-Philippe. To accommodate the imperial tomb inside the Dome, the architect Visconti conducted significant excavation work. This was a sign of the respect that the French people had for Napoleon — a respect that was not only hard earned but well-earned.

Chapter Summary

- June 22nd, 1815 — Napoleon confronted the harsh reality of abdication in Paris.
- June 25th, 1815 — Napoleon left Paris, and sought solace in Malmaison, eventually bidding his mother farewell.
- June 31st, 1815 — News of his exile to Saint. Helena — a remote island under British rule in the Atlantic Ocean — reached Napoleon while he was at the port of Plymouth.
- August 7-9th — Napoleon boarded the Northumberland and left British shores.
- October 15th, 1815 — Napoleon arrived on the desolate island of Saint. Helena.
- 1818-1819 — Several of Napoleon's friends left the island. He grew increasingly lonely.
- May 5th, 1821 — Napoleon died at the age of 51 from what was probably stomach cancer (though some historians have speculated that he was poisoned).

Segue

Napoleon's life is, perhaps, so fascinating because he started as an underdog from Corsica, rose to great power, and then had a great fall. It's the sort of "Humpty Dumpty" story that draws people in and keeps them enchanted from beginning to end. There's a reason why they're still making movies about Napoleon Bonaparte centuries later, after all. In the next section, we'll be wrapping things up and talking about everything we've learned so far. This will be a great opportunity to take a comprehensive look at the lasting mark that Napoleon left on European history.

Conclusion

Napoleon had a huge impact on France, no doubt about it. As a leader in the military and politics, he made some major changes. He came up with the Napoleonic Code, which not only modernized legal systems but also laid the groundwork for the principles of equality and individual rights. He didn't stop there, though — his grand plans stretched across Europe, and he set up the French Empire, completely changing how things looked on the map. Of course, he did hit a roadblock when he tried to invade Great Britain. This had a major effect on European history, especially in terms of naval power.

Napoleon wasn't just shaking things up in Europe, however; he also changed how wars were fought in general. His clever battle strategies, like focusing on moving fast and making quick decisions, to give you a few examples, influenced military leaders for a long time, even during the American Civil War and the early days of World War I. The "Napoleonic style" of warfare was studied by military leaders all over the world — and still is being studied today by historians.

Of course, we can't gloss over his Russian campaign, which went about as badly as it could have. This period in his life showed that even someone as brilliant as Napoleon had his weak spots. His troops couldn't handle the harsh Russian winter and the rough terrain — clearly, he wasn't as invincible as he thought he was. His retreat from Moscow (and abandonment of his troops) was a turning point in European history for sure.

What perhaps makes Napoleon so interesting is his personality. He was a genius in the military and had big ideas as a leader, but he was also a complicated person with flaws. People were drawn to his charm, ambition, and talent for getting people to stick by him no matter what (until, of course, the European powers united against him). Although he could be practical, a lot of people were scared of him. It's widely agreed that his eagerness for power eventually led to his downfall.

After his death, Napoleon's family took charge across Europe, mainly achieving power through alliances and marriages. This was exactly what Napoleon wanted — for his relatives to create a web of powerful connections. Even though Napoleon's era ended with him losing at Waterloo in 1815, the effects of his rule and his family's ambitions will continue to echo throughout European history. Napoleon's legacy today is a mixture of spectacular wins and crushing losses, which just goes to show how complicated his impact has been on the world as a whole.

If you enjoyed this book, please feel free to leave a review or share it with your history-inclined friends. Remember, there's a lot of incorrect information out there about Napoleon, and I've done everything I can to provide you with the facts in this book. Napoleon Bonaparte's legacy will surely live on forever, and it's interesting to think about how he would react to Europe (and the world) as it is now.

Resources

1769-1793: Napoleon Bonaparte's early years - napoleon.org. (n.d.). napoleon.org. https://www.napoleon.org/en/history-of-the-two-empires/timelines/1769-1793-napoleon-bonapartes-early-years/#:~:text=Napoleon%20was%20born%20on%2015,20%2C000%20Francs%20in%20Napoleon's%20will

ABC News. (2007, January 17). What killed Napoleon? *ABC News.* https://abcnews.go.com/Technology/story?id=2802454&page=1

ARCE. (2023, February 11). *The Rosetta Stone: Unlocking the Ancient Egyptian Language - ARCE.* https://arce.org/resource/rosetta-stone-unlocking-ancient-egyptian-language/#:~:text=With%20the%20mysteries%20of%20the,of%20king%20Ptolemy%20V%20Epiphanes

Brown Bess or Charleville? | napoleonicwars. (2020, May 10). Napoleonicwars. https://www.thenapoleonicwars.net/forum/general-discussions/brown-bess-or-charleville

Da Costa, J. (2022, January 7). How Napoleon turned the official painting of his coronation into a propaganda tool. *Medium.* https://medium.com/the-collector/how-napoleon-turned-the-official-painting-of-his-coronation-into-a-propaganda-tool-bfc9f83a480b

Egyptian campaign. (n.d.). National Army Museum. https://www.nam.ac.uk/explore/egyptian-campaign

Empress Josephine (1763-1814) - Napoleon.org. (n.d.). napoleon.org. https://www.napoleon.org/en/young-historians/napodoc/limperatrice-josephine-1763-1814/

French Revolutionary wars | Causes, Combatants, & Battles. (1998, July 20). Encyclopedia Britannica. https://www.britannica.com/event/French-revolutionary-wars/Formation-of-the-Second-Coalition

From Waterloo to the island of St Helena - napoleon.org. (n.d.). napoleon.org. https://www.napoleon.org/en/young-historians/napodoc/from-waterloo-to-the-island-of-st-helena/#:~:text=Napoleon%20died%20on%205%20May,caused%20by%20a%20stomach%20ulcer

Greenspan, J. (2023, August 11). *Why Napoleon's invasion of Russia was the beginning of the end.* HISTORY. https://www.history.com/news/napoleons-disastrous-invasion-of-russia

History of Europe | Summary, Wars, Map, Ideas, & Colonialism. (2023, October 20). Encyclopedia Britannica. https://www.britannica.com/topic/history-of-Europe/The-Napoleonic-era

Knighton, A. (2017, July 6). *He Started As An Artillery Officer And Became An Emperor – The Spectacular Rise Of Napoleon.* Warhistoryonline. https://www.warhistoryonline.com/napoleon/4-steps-napoleons-rise-power-m.html

Lowndes, C. (2020, December 18). Napoleon's missing hand, explained. *Vox.* https://www.vox.com/2020/12/18/22189148/napoleons-missing-hand-explained#:~:text=The%20answer%20is%20rooted%20in,way%20to%20speak%20in%20public

MARIE-LOUISE OF AUSTRIA - *Napoleon.org*. (n.d.). napoleon.org. https://www.napoleon.org/en/history-of-the-two-empires/biographies/marie-louise-of-austria/

Mark, H. W. (2023a). Napoleon's campaign in Egypt and Syria. *World History Encyclopedia*. https://www.worldhistory.org/Napoleon's_Campaign_in_Egypt_and_Syria/

Mark, H. W. (2023b). Coronation of Napoleon I. *World History Encyclopedia*. https://www.worldhistory.org/article/2251/coronation-of-napoleon-i/

Mark, H. W. (2023c). Napoleon's Invasion of Russia. *World History Encyclopedia*. https://www.worldhistory.org/Napoleon's_Invasion_of_Russia/

Mark, H. W. (2023d). Napoleon's Italian campaign. *World History Encyclopedia*. https://www.worldhistory.org/Napoleon's_Italian_Campaign/

Martyris, N. (2015, June 18). Appetite For War: What Napoleon And His Men Ate On The March. *NPR*. https://www.npr.org/sections/thesalt/2015/06/18/414614705/appetite-for-war-what-napoleon-and-his-men-ate-on-the-march

McLean, J. (n.d.). *Napoleon's Marriage to Marie-Louise | History of Western Civilization II*. https://courses.lumenlearning.com/suny-hccc-worldhistory2/chapter/napoleons-marriage-to-marie-louise/

Napoleon and Josephine. (n.d.). https://www.napoleon-series.org/research/napoleon/c_napjos.html

Napoleon Bonaparte | OSU eHistory. (n.d.). https://ehistory.osu.edu/biographies/napoleon-bonaparte

Napoleon Bonaparte - Biography, Facts & Death | HISTORY. (2009, November 9). *HISTORY.*
https://www.history.com/topics/european-history/napoleon

Napoleon Bonaparte, student of the Royal Military School in Brienne, aged 15 years old - napoleon.org. (n.d.). napoleon.org.
https://www.napoleon.org/en/history-of-the-two-empires/objects/napoleon-bonaparte-student-of-the-royal-military-school-in-brienne-aged-15-years-old/

Napoleon Bonaparte Study Guide: Exile and Escape | SparkNotes. (n.d.). SparkNotes.
https://www.sparknotes.com/biography/napoleon/section9/#:~:text=On%20February%2026%2C%201815%2C%20Napoleon,rally%20to%20the%20returned%20Emperor

Napoleon crowned emperor. (2010, March 4). *HISTORY.*
https://www.history.com/this-day-in-history/napoleon-crowned-emperor

Napoleon I | Biography, Achievements, & Facts. (2023, November 19). Encyclopedia Britannica.
https://www.britannica.com/biography/Napoleon-I/The-Directory

Napoleonic satires. (n.d.).
https://library.brown.edu/cds/napoleon/time6.html

Napoleon's "Grande Armée" (1) - Napoleon.org. (n.d.). napoleon.org.
https://www.napoleon.org/en/young-historians/napodoc/napoleons-grande-armee-1/

Napoleon's Rise & Fall: Illustrated Timeline – Virginia Museum of Fine Arts |. (n.d.). https://vmfa.museum/learn/resources/napoleons-rise-fall-illustrated-timeline/

National Gallery of Victoria. (n.d.-a). *Napoleon > Napoleon in Egypt.* Copyright (C) 2013 National Gallery of Victoria.

https://www.ngv.vic.gov.au/napoleon/facts-and-figures/napoleon-in-egypt.html

National Gallery of Victoria. (n.d.-b). *Napoleon > The Italian Campaigns*. Copyright (C) 2013 National Gallery of Victoria. https://www.ngv.vic.gov.au/napoleon/facts-and-figures/the-italian-campaigns.html

National Gallery of Victoria. (n.d.-c). *Napoleon > Who was Josephine?* Copyright (C) 2013 National Gallery of Victoria. https://www.ngv.vic.gov.au/napoleon/napoleon-and-josephine/who-was-josephine.html

The Editors of Encyclopaedia Britannica. (1998, July 20). *Siege of Toulon | Facts, summary, & Napoleon Bonaparte*. Encyclopedia Britannica. https://www.britannica.com/event/Siege-of-Toulon

The Editors of Encyclopaedia Britannica. (2023, October 27). *Hundred Days | Napoleon, Waterloo, Reforms*. Encyclopedia Britannica. https://www.britannica.com/event/Hundred-Days-French-history

Timeline of the 100 days - age of Revolution. (2015, January 20). Age of Revolution. https://ageofrevolution.org/themes/battle/timeline-of-the-100-days/

Times, N. Y. (2002, June 23). "Napoleon: a Biography." *The New York Times*. https://www.nytimes.com/2002/06/23/books/chapters/napoleon-a-biography.html

Unification of Italian States - Countries - Office of the Historian. (n.d.). https://history.state.gov/countries/issues/italian-unification

Warfare History Network. (2022, September 1). *Napoleon's stunning debut: The Italian Campaign - Warfare History Network*. https://warfarehistorynetwork.com/article/napoleons-stunning-debut-the-italian-campaign/

Printed in Great Britain
by Amazon